**FRIENDS OF AC**

W9-DBI-016

2  20·74

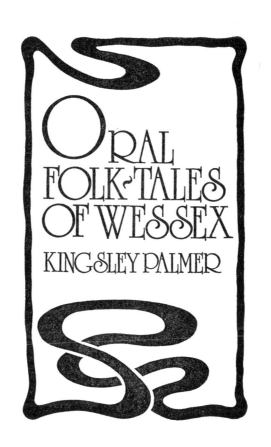

# ORAL FOLK-TALES OF WESSEX

### KINGSLEY PALMER

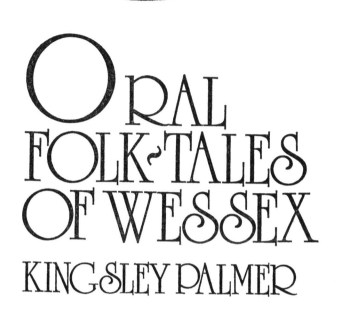

# ORAL FOLK·TALES OF WESSEX

## KINGSLEY PALMER

DAVID & CHARLES    NEWTON ABBOT

0 7153 5905 3

Set in 11 on 13pt Baskerville
and printed in Great Britain
by Latimer Trend & Company Ltd Plymouth
for David & Charles (Holdings) Limited
South Devon House   Newton Abbot   Devon

1788237

To

My Mother and Father

# CONTENTS

INTRODUCTORY                                      *page* 9

1  SETTLEMENT AND DWELLING                         13

2  LIVELIHOOD AND HOUSEHOLD SUPPORT                 27

3  COMMUNICATION AND TRADE                          36

4  THE COMMUNITY                                    43

5  HUMAN LIFE                                       58

6  NATURE                                           69

7  FOLK MEDICINE AND TIME                           81

8  POPULAR BELIEF AND PRACTICE                      93

9  MYTHOLOGICAL TRADITIONS: 1                       104

10  MYTHOLOGICAL TRADITIONS: 2                      131

11  HISTORICAL TRADITIONS                           155

   NOTES                                            169

   CLASSIFICATION OF ORAL TALES AND
      TRADITIONS                                    176

   BIBLIOGRAPHY                                     186

   ACKNOWLEDGEMENTS                                 191

   INDEX                                            193

# INTRODUCTORY

Oral traditions belong to us all and like our own pasts are present reminders of how we or our forebears used to think and believe. This collection of tales and traditions from Wessex represents many of the stories told by its inhabitants and demonstrates what was in the minds and mouths of its people at the time of collection. These tales are told partly for fun, for entertainment or even in half belief, and they are presented here as they were collected, without the embroidery which many collected versions of oral tales have suffered. Background information and relevant facts have been added where such clarification is necessary, along with some examination of the implications of tradition, transmission and transmutation.

The area of the study has been broadly called 'Wessex'. Tales are included from Wiltshire, Gloucestershire, Dorset, Somerset, Devon and Cornwall, with a few examples from farther afield. The book is the continuation of a detailed survey of south Somerset and central Dorset so that these two areas are particularly well represented. Most village settlements have their own oral traditions and a complete survey of the six counties listed above would be a considerable undertaking. It seemed wise therefore to present a detailed and accurate survey of a relatively small area, and then by comparison extend the scope of the study to similar areas studied in rather less detail. The initial survey established that the two rural areas of Somerset and Dorset produced a variety of traditions surprisingly similar in nature, and the material taken from areas beyond these demonstrated that this similarity extended through Wessex. As place names are always mentioned the reader may enjoy comparing his own knowledge of local traditions with those in areas with which he is perhaps unfamiliar. The book thus aims to study traditions widely through Wessex, rather than in several particular areas.

The survey was conducted by the author between 1968 and 1970. It was systematic and in the Somerset area in particular

9

it endeavoured to reach all who could usefully provide information within a specified area limit. Tales and traditions were either taped and later transcribed, or written down as told. Both these methods reduce the possibility of extraneous material being introduced by the author at a later stage, or important details being left out. The details of the interviews, dates, times and conditions, along with brief biographical details of the informants were also noted, and all material was classified and stored for later examination. The aim was to interview everybody who could possibly be of help in the specified areas, and while it is certain that many must have been overlooked, it was intended to collect as many as possible of the oral traditions extant, under scientific conditions. This would help to obviate the woolly mindedness and casual thinking that has for too long marked the folklorist as a pseudo-scientist.

Material collected in this survey has been indented in the text, and should be regarded as being as nearly as is possible a reproduction of what an informant had to say. For obvious reasons the details of the informants are not given, though the source for additional material is given in the notes.

Classification is always a difficulty. Academic study necessitates some system for experts, but to the general reader its presence adds nothing, and very often spoils good reading. The difficulties in the choice of the system, its adaptation and compilation will therefore be passed over. It is hoped that this system, to be found on page 176, based on that suggested by Sean O'Suilleabhain in his book *A Handbook of Irish Folklore*, itself an adaptation of the Uppsala system, will be of use to other collectors. It will make all material accessible to the student of the folktale, while remaining more or less unobtrusive to the general reader.

Obviously some tales and traditions, details and comments have had to be omitted; some of course were missed in the surveys. What is to be found in the following pages is therefore a sample of a vast area of uncollected and unconsidered traditions. This collection demonstrates that while some areas of belief are certainly dying, others are being retained with tenacity, and being added to in certain instances. These stories told, it seems, for entertainment will entertain the reader as they did when first handed on, but their hold over the backwaters of man's spiritual development retains a contemporary significance offering far more than mere entertainment.

# CHAPTER 1

# SETTLEMENT AND DWELLING

## A.1. Local settlers

In some places traditions have survived concerning an early settler. Often the settler was a missionary who according to legend was badly treated, and perhaps even murdered. A good example of this story is still to be found around Watchet in Somerset. The parish church at Watchet is called after the saint who is reputed to have founded it, St Decuman. According to tradition St Decuman came across the sea on a hurdle or even a faggot, while some say that it was on his cloak. A cow came with him and fed him with her milk. After he had landed he looked for the first hill that he could see, and there built a church. However, local opposition to him was strong, and eventually he was beheaded. The action was in vain, as he simply picked up his head, washed the blood in a nearby stream, and went away, back across the sea.

The story has been collected in several different versions. Hutton mentions it much as it is given above.[1] Certainly the spring or holy well is still to be seen due west of the church on the side of a steep slope, and now much overgrown. Camden gives us the following account.

> S. Decombes, who setting sail out of south Wales, landed here [Watchet] (as we find it in an ancient Agonel) 'in a horrid desert full of shrubs and briars, the wood thick and close, stretched out in a vast way both in length and breadth, strutting up with lofty mountains, sever'd wonderfully by the hollow vallies'. Here having bid farewell to the vanities of the world, he was stab'd by an assassin, and so got the reputation of a saint among the common people.[2]

There are variations in the story, especially as regards the means employed by the saint to cross the sea. E. Boger records that he came over on a cloak,[3] whereas Walters has it that he came on the back of an ox.[4] C. H. Poole tells us that he was killed in AD 706, and that his festival is on 27 August. He was killed by 'a pagan inhabitant' who 'severed his head from his shoulders . . . the head was by the body carried away and washed in a spring in which he was accostomed to bathe'.[5]

St Decuman was most probably a Romanised Briton who was active as a missionary and whose influence spread over parts of north Somerset, west Cornwall and south Wales.[6]

One of the most striking aspects of the story is the beheading and the miraculous survival. The theme is a well known one, and occurs in *Sir Gawain and the Green Knight* to mention only one instance, though in this case the theme may have come from a French source. Here, however, is a completely magical incident, unsophisticated yet powerfully maintained. The well that survives is naturally a healing or holy well.

That missionaries were active in early years throughout Wessex is underlined by another story that comes from Crewkerne. A hill near the town is called Rayn Hill, and local tradition has it that there was an old church or dwelling place there, inhabited by St Rayn. This saint was probably associated with St Reigne of Reginfrede, Bishop of Cologne, who with St Boniface, the apostle of the Germans, and fifty more were martyred on Whitsun eve, AD 775. These were mostly Wessex men sent as missionaries, and their martyrdom was commemorated at Whitsuntide annually. 'It can be assumed therefore that St Rayne was venerated in the fifteenth century in a chapel or cell near Crewkerne.'[7]

R. Hunt collected a story that contains the same motif of magical transportation of a saint across the sea, though in this case the evil was done to the saint by the Irish, and it was the Cornishmen who treated him well. St Piran, so the story goes, had been very kind to the kings of Ireland, but the kings condemned him to be cast into the sea with a huge millstone round his neck. The day was rough and the sea tempestuous, but as soon as he was pushed over the cliff the wind died down and the sea became calm. Hundreds were converted to Christianity as they saw this miracle. St Piran floated safely to Cornwall where he landed on 5 March on the sands that are now called after him. He lived in Cornwall until he reached the age of 206.[8]

*A.2. Derivations of the names of villages and places*
While early settlers have contributed to oral tradition, a more obvious response has come from that which is more a part of everyday life. An example of such is the explanations that have been circulated describing the origins of the names of places. A small village near Ilminster, Somerset, called Allowenshay was found to have a variety of explanations for its unusual name. Altogether eight different versions of the same tradition were recorded. The idea was that during a war at some time or other, forage for the horses came from the place—or the 'allowance of hay'—thus Allowenshay. Stories collected differed only in detail. Some stated that it dated from the time of the Monmouth rebellion, and others that it was the time of the battle of Sedgemoor. Some said that it was in the 'old days', or 'olden times'. One informant updated it to the time of World War I. In a further version there was an implied insult, typical of the stories told about another village. This was that the hay had

to be rationed and 'allowanced out' because they could not grow much hay there.

In fact the name comes from 'Aepelwine's enclosure . . . (ge)haeg—hay, enclosed piece of land, meadow. ME hay also forest fenced off for hunting',[9] and is pronounced 'Allunzay'.

Sometimes the explanation is little more than a crude pun. The name Dundry has provided us with a story about an architect who built the towers of Chew Magna, Chewton Mendip and Dundry. When he had completed the last of the three he is supposed to have said, 'Now I have *done dree.*'

Dorset provides a variety of tales to explain the origin of the names Child Okeford, Shillingstone and Okeford Fitzpaine. Three versions of a similar story were collected, explaining that a long time ago a baby was found abandoned—usually in the church porch at Shillingstone. The elders from the three villages met to decide what they should do with the child. Shillingstone contributed a shilling, Okeford Fitzpaine gave five pence. It was originally called Okeford Fifepenny. Child Okeford undertook to rear the child. Slight variations are found in the story, but the pattern is generally established. An informant from Wiltshire told me that he had heard a similar story about Sixpenny Handley. (The true derivations of the names concerned may be found in E. Ekwall, *Concise Oxford Dictionary of English Place-Names.*)

Some pieces of folk etymology are quite obvious in their explanation. One informant explained that the name Oxenford came from it being a place where the oxen crossed the river (correct), while another explained Whitelackington as being a place where there must have been a white lake at some time or other (but it means the settlement of the son of Whitlac). One of the most charming stories of all explains a small country lane near Taunton, called Badger Street. The old story about how it earned such a strange name, an informant told me, was that all through the badgers' mating season, all the badgers from the Blackdowns used to come down through Staple Fitzpaine, and the ones from the Brendons used to come down the other way, and they used to meet there to choose their wives.

The badgers from the Blackdowns were the males and those from the Brendons were the females.

These kinds of tradition are widespread and retain popularity. Some even contain a note of erudition. Seavington St Michael produced the following piece of folk etymology. The name originated from the fact that the village is twenty miles from the sea, 'Sea-vingt-ton,' ie, the settlement twenty miles from the sea. Its true etymology is given as 'C. 1025, Seafenempton. D.B. Seovenamentone—"The tun of the Soefonhaeme, or dwellers at a locality called 'Seven Wells' or the like." '[10]

Finally, Bolsover in Derbyshire gives us an example of an imaginative etymology. When Cromwell attacked the castle during the Civil War and fired cannon up at the town, the inhabitants cried, 'the balls are over', and that is how the town got its name.

### A.2.i. Stories of local landowners and people

Local landowners have frequently been regarded with a kind of suspicion by their tenants and the more lowly inhabitants of an area. Stories of their eccentricities frequently pass into oral tradition, exhibiting many of the usual features of exaggeration and mystery that so typifies that oral tradition. One story collected from Somerset told of a feud between two local landowners. This resulted in a fight that took place in a local park, and eventually the dispute was settled in Star Chamber. The tradition as it is current in oral sources has a literary parallel, and indeed the former probably came from the latter.[11] The discrepancy between the probable source and the oral tradition as found points to the traits of the process of reassimilation by a literate folk of literary material. This process is constituting a valuable new oral tradition.

Associated with this last tradition and from the same village is the story that as a result of the feud the two families would not go into the village church by the same door. Thus a new door was built and can still be seen, though now bricked up. This is similar to the story explaining why there are two churches at the Somerset village of Stocklinch. Two sisters, the story goes, had an argument and refused to attend the same church. Thus another church was built, so that they could worship in separate buildings.

Often, however, stories tell of the eccentricities of the landed gentry. The story is told of a rather unstable man called Pitt, who lived at Cricket Court, Ilminster, and one night went around and shot the portraits of all his ancestors. It was also said that he had a special room upstairs where he kept his coffin. Of course the tradition continues to tell of how he haunted the place. We know that the Pitts had acquired the house by 1623, and by Collinson's time (1791) the whole parish belonged to Stephen Pitt. The present building has the crest of Admiral Pitt, and is dated 1790. The earlier building is presumed to have burned down. Admiral Pitt is presumably the eccentric one, as he built the whole house to resemble a ship inside, which indeed it does, and he was responsible for the building of a recess in an upstairs room for his coffin. The family line became extinct in 1930.

Since in this case we have certain factual evidence to work on, some conclusions may be drawn. First, the traditions of Pitt's eccentricities have survived from a little after 1790, and are still widely told in the area. Secondly, it serves to illustrate the typical folk reaction to upper-class society, where the modes of behaviour were so far removed from their own that a tale for entertainment and astonishment resulted.

Traditions of landowners often, indeed, contain the idea that they were somehow sinister people, out of this world. A story collected about Charborough Park, Dorset, told how the lady of the house would appear while the local children were gathering daffodils from the woods; she would spy on them and was supposed to be a witch. Once, when picking blackberries, the children saw the woman and then watched as she suddenly vanished into thin air. Workmen in the park told similar stories, and people kept out of her way for fear of receiving the 'evil eye'.

The gap between the landed gentry and the labourers has been responsible for the way the gentry in folk tradition inhabit a separate planet, their actions—admittedly sometimes extravagant—not being understood. There is inherent in the tradition a subconscious note of indictment by the folk at the imbalance of the social order. In each case the tradition shows some criticism of the situation, however mildly this is expressed.

Charborough House provides one more story that is simple and charming in itself. If it does anything it explains the classical statues at the Lion Lodge entrance to the grounds. Many years ago the daughter of Charborough House fell in love with a mere labourer, and the marriage was strongly opposed by the father, who forbade them to meet. But the couple did so in secret at the extreme edge of the park at Lion Lodge. When the father discovered this, he ordered that statues of nude men be placed at the lodge to shame the daughter. This trick worked, and she was so embarrassed that she refused to go to Lion Lodge, and thus was not able to see her boy-friend. Years later, after her father had died, when she too was on her death-bed, she made a will saying that the statues should have fig leaves placed on them, to stop any further embarrassment, and to allow people to meet there without shame.

*A.4 Villages, stories of growth, situations and buildings*
The past haunts present oral tales and traditions with a constant mystery. People love to hear of lost villages and buried towns. A tradition widespread across the Blackdown Hills told of a city that was once built there, called Cityford; it was destroyed in a war many years ago, and the gates of the city were taken off to France. Similarly there is the lost village of Easenton, supposed to have lain off the coast of Watchet and washed away by the sea many years ago. However, the bell of the village church is said still to be heard tolling when there is a deep undersea swell, and this is taken as a supernatural warning of bad weather to come.[12]

In Milton Abbas, Dorset, submarine bells are supposed to be heard every New Year's Eve. This is the anniversary of the flooding of the old village to please the whim of a new landlord, who, wanting to see a lake from his windows and not a village, flooded the valley and rehoused his labourers out of sight up a small valley. In fact the result was the well-planned and pleasing village so much visited today.

The notion that landowners' parks have consumed villages is expressed in a tradition from Somerset of Hinton House. One informant remembered his father saying, as he pointed to the park, 'There's a town out there buried.' Certainly in more general terms folk traditions are concerned about the origin and history of their towns and villages. One wonders if villages swallowed up by airfields and reservoirs will produce similar stories. A rhyme concerning Norton Fitzwarren expresses the feeling that it was a settlement long before Taunton and perhaps dates from times when the two places could consider themselves rivals.

> Norton was a busy town
> When Taunton was a vuzzy down.

This should be compared with the rhyme concerning Crediton and Exeter:

> Kerdon was a market town
> When Exeter was a vuzzy down.

or the Plympton and Plymouth version:

> When Plympton was a busy town
> Plymouth was a vuzzy down
> Now Plymouth is a busy town
> And Plympton is a vuzzy down.[18]

Poole in Dorset offers a final example:

> Poole was a thriving town
> When Liverpool was a furzy down.

*A.5. Lucky or unlucky sites for houses, materials, traditions and building procedure*

Traditions relating to houses and buildings are diverse. Some houses or areas are considered to be unlucky, often as a result of a curse. Such traditions will be dealt with under the appropriate section (see pp 97–102). Other traditions, however, quite simply record the fact that some sort of bad luck or good luck is associated with a particular situation. An informant from Stourpaine, Dorset, indicated that the old hill forts of Hod and Hambledon hills protected the villages of Durweston and Stourpaine that lie close to these hills by some supernatural force. By contrast, an area in the village of Broadway, Somerset, has the local reputation for bringing ill luck on all who work there. Certainly no one in living memory has prospered there.

Much of the tradition accumulating round building procedure rests on the fact that frequently new houses were built from the stone of former buildings or derelict structures near by. This, in itself, can lead to beliefs implying that the stone was obtained by strange and unexplained means. An informant said of Donyatt, Somerset, that all the stone for the houses in the village was taken locally, but that there was no stone quarry there; this is partly explained by the information given by another informant, that the village was redeveloped in the 1880s. The old mansion house was pulled down in 1877, '. . . and the stones used for the construction of farm buildings'.[14] This pattern of development also holds true for nearby Hilcombe; the stone for Bellmoor farm was taken from a nearby house, Hilcombe Walls. In fact the date on the cottage fits well with the time when, we can deduce, the old house either fell into disuse or was burnt down.[15]

The traditions develop where there is more mystery associated with the source of the stones. West Dowlish once had a church, but now all that is left above ground is a graveyard. The stones from the old church were almost certainly used by local builders; in fact in one house near the old church a builder discovered some cut, blackened stone inside a wall. There were other traces of cut stone that had obviously come from the church, which had in all probability been burned down.

Sometimes it is clear that stones from an old building have been incorporated in its successor for reasons beyond economy or convenience. The Minster Church, Boscastle, in Cornwall, provides an excellent example. On the south side of the tower at a height of about 14ft is an oblong piece of stone carved in a particular way. It is set as a part of the structure of the tower, and is almost indistinguishable from the other stone blocks. On investigation this stone is clearly a cut section of a carved archway top such as is to be found on the arch top of the tower windows. Further, the gateway entrance to the churchyard was found to have a small wall capped by another piece of carved stone, similar though retaining its original shape. Someone had taken a good deal of trouble to carve a former window arch into a solid oblong stone, and set it obviously in the tower. During some restoration of the church, old stone was naturally re-used, and the builders ensured that this fact was made known. Church stone is consecrated, and the builders were taking care that the stone was not used for a baser purpose, as well as that the virtue the old stone possessed was perpetuated in the new structure. This is a continuation of the process whereby significant parts of pagan buildings were included, usually quite inconspicuously, in their Christian counterparts. Incidentally, the tower of the Minster Church also has a strange scissor mark on its west side, usually interpreted as a mason's mark, and in the grounds of the church lie the remains of an old priory that also might have provided stone for rebuilding.

*A.7. House luck*

Sometimes specific houses are known in local tradition for their good or bad luck. As with more general locations accredited with a curse, this is usually the result of one specific incident, or a series of incidents that have marked the place out as being either good or bad. One of the most interesting examples I have come across is a modern one, concerning a public house near Blandford Forum, Dorset. The place was once three cottages, the middle one being an off-licence. The owner wanted to expand this into a public house. One of the three cottages was to be converted, and the occupant to move into an upstairs flat. The occupant at first agreed to the change but then changed his mind, and became so upset with the landlord that he went out and drowned himself in the River Stour. The landlady later died of cancer and the occupant of the other cottage cut her throat with a razor for no apparent reason. (Her husband complained that she had used his best razor to do it.)

The next landlord converted the whole place into a pub, but he dropped dead at a darts match. The wife of the landlord after him said that she could hear the ghost of the man who drowned himself moving about. The landlord later committed suicide in Blandford Church by taking an overdose of aspirins —this last incident is certainly true, as the local police will testify. It has led to the belief amongst local schoolchildren that his ghost now haunts the church. The body, in fact, was not discovered until some time after death, and the church was later reconsecrated.

There is now little local feeling in the area concerning the house, probably because the pub has changed its name, and the change, it is thought, could be accompanied by a change in the luck. However, recently a further instalment has been added to the story—that a woman hanged herself from a beam in the main bar of the pub. As the ceiling height is only just over 6ft, and the beams considerably less, she must have been a very short lady to achieve this. The present occupants of the inn admit to hearing some noises at night, but they do not think that these result from any sort of ghost. Certainly the tradition seems to have little effect on the thirst of the locals.

Bad house luck may be countered by certain folk charms. A bullock's heart, placed in the chimney, was always held to be efficacious against the entry of evil spirits (via the chimney) or witches, though use of an onion or even bacon has been reported.[16] Most objects were stuck through with pins or thorns. The horseshoe is a usual charm against bad house luck.

One story from Dorset told of a tightly corked bottle that was found hanging by a wire inside a chimney; when removed it was found to contain some liquid, but the bottle was broken and the liquid ran away. Afterwards the family experienced nothing but bad luck, and eventually were forced to leave the farmhouse. A small bottle of mercury carried in the pocket is said to ward off the evil eye.

*A.9.ii. Giants' graves*

People living near ancient burial chambers have frequently explained them as 'giants' graves'. While there is little doubt that these mounds were in most cases burial sites, the tradition that previous inhabitants of an area were by nature giants is less rational! Five traditions were collected from Somerset concerning a 'giant's grave' near Bishop's Wood. This is of interest because the mound is now levelled, leaving no signs, and the traditions of the area have become little more than a casual statement about a giant's grave. R. Tongue sheds some light and much confusion on this tradition when she writes, 'There is a place called the Devil's Stone at Ham Lane, and another at Combe St Nicholas, but my parents always said that it was the grave of a giant who fought the Devil and got killed, and was buried where the roads meet to stop him from walking.'[17] There is in fact no devil's stone at Combe St Nicholas that I have been able to locate, and since Miss Tongue's information is dated as 1961 it seems unlikely that the oral traditions, so strong elsewhere, should have died out so soon. It seems more probable that Miss Tongue has credited Combe St Nicholas with both a stone and a devil that it never had; it does however seem likely that the story concerns the giant's grave near Bishop's Wood, though its location would include it in the parish of Combe St Nicholas. Grinsell lists *Giant's Grave*, Combe St Nicholas, and states that it 'is now destroyed and the only evidence for it is the memory of the old inhabitants who told the late A. T. Wicks that it was a long mound, but with the larger end at the west, and not (as is more usual in long barrows) to the east'. It is situated 'by Giant's Grave Road. The name attests the former existence of folklore.' It is listed finally as 'Combe St Nicholas 1. Site of possible destroyed long barrow'.[18]

This giant's grave is typical of the links that objects like long barrows made with oral tradition, and further illustrates that the removal of the object is the first stage in the removal of the oral tradition.

A somewhat similar tale is told of the Giant's Grave at Cheselborne, Dorset. The story goes that two giants were standing on an adjacent hill and were having a stone-throwing contest. The giant who lost the contest was so disgruntled that he died of despair and was buried beneath the mound, since called 'Giant's Grave'.[19] A similar story is told of the origin of Nor-dun (near Nettlecombe Toot) by Mr Warne in *Ancient Dorset*, p 83. (This story is also mentioned by Udal, p 162.)

*A.9.xii. Other places where people have been buried, including crossroads*
The extensive oral tradition collected about burial at crossroads rests on the fundamental belief that if a person dies in suspicious circumstances (usually suicide) or was a murderer, his ghost is likely to be troublesome. It was therefore thought necessary to bury the corpse by or under a crossroads, with a stake through the heart to prevent the corpse 'walking'. It was also usual to bury a suicide in unconsecrated ground; thus a suitable spot outside the churchyard had to be found. A small suicide's grave near Manton on Dartmoor is known as 'Jay's grave' and is supposed to be the grave of a little servant girl. In Suffolk is 'Boy's grave', situated by the wayside at a crossroads between Newmarket and Bury St Edmunds. The story behind this grave is that a shepherd boy thought he had lost one of his sheep, and in despair, afraid that he would be hanged for sheep-stealing, committed suicide. Later it was found that he had not lost a sheep and had merely miscounted.[20]

In Somerset a large number of traditions were collected concerning Mary Hunt's grave, near Ilminster. Altogether seventeen versions of the tale were collected. Some said that Mary Hunt was a gipsy, others that she committed suicide, or that she was a witch, one that she was a prostitute, another that she killed herself because she was going to have a baby. Naturally in some versions the crossroads became haunted. One informant added that people used to say that between 12 o'clock and 1 o'clock Mary Hunt would rattle her chains—rattle her chains and turn in her grave—but the informant had never heard anything himself.

There were also some variations in descriptions of the manner of appearance. One said that she came down 'on a kind of trolley', while another said that she would be seen doing her knitting, as she was doing her knitting when she was murdered. This strange piece of information is complemented by a similar tradition from Dorset. An informant at Wool told me that there was, on the road to West Lulworth, about a mile from Wool, a tree called 'Grandma's Knitting Tree', where the ghost of a woman knitting could be seen.

A similar body of tradition surrounds a crossroads near Crewkerne, called Nan Bull's Grave. Once again, opinion varies as to the exact origin of 'Nan Bull', but we do know that Mary Ann Bull was a lone gipsy who travelled round selling trinkets. She was rather too fond of the bottle, but local inhabitants, particularly in Dorset, were afraid of her power to curse. One informant from Dorset could remember seeing Nan Bull when she was a child, for she often camped in her waggon in a field near his home. O. Knott in *Witches of Wessex* (pp 11–14) tells us that she was eventually found dead beneath her cart, at the side of the road near Yeovil. The inquest was held at Wincanton, where she was also, presumably, buried. Nevertheless, tradition has sprung up in comparatively recent years about the event, and established a strong oral tradition that relates this historical character to a geographical situation.

There are of course many other crossroad-grave traditions; reference could be made to Cannard's Grave[21] and Merland's Corner.[22] From Cornwall, R. Hunt collected a story of the same tradition, including an explanation of the name Spearman—the man who put the spear through the suicide's heart, to stop him walking.[23]

# CHAPTER 2

# LIVELIHOOD AND HOUSEHOLD SUPPORT

## B.2.ii. Poaching

The theme of poaching has quite naturally a popular appeal in folklore. Not only was poaching a serious means of supplementing an otherwise meagre diet, but it was also a way in which some people could claim a part of what they felt was in any case their rightful property. The immediate appeal of many of the stories rests on the success of the poachers against the powers of the establishment. On the darker side the stories usually take place at night, and there is the idea that after all the action was wrong, a form of stealing, and in any case subject to severe penalties. No psychological theory is needed to explain the guilty's greater preoccupation with the accusing shadows and threatening night sounds. A woodland or heath can be a frightening place under normal circumstances after dark, without the thought of a gamekeeper or landowner who was willing to shoot first and ask questions after. Thus the stories are a mixture of a type of smug contentment and of exhibitions of mysterious incidents in the dark, some obviously stemming from a guilty conscience.

Folklore has romanticised the social struggle represented by poaching, and thereby excluded many of the grimmer realities of the action. Sheep-stealing was of course a penal offence, and partly as a result of the stiff penalties no doubt the violence shown in the avoidance of arrest was considerable. With large areas of land controlled by landowners and patrolled by gamekeepers, the struggle between law and poacher has been a long and bloody one. John of Salisbury, a contemporary of Henry II, writes:

> They are not afraid for the sake of a brute beast to destroy a human being whom the Son of God redeemed with his own blood. They dare in God's sight to claim as their own property the wild creatures . . . and it is often held as a crime to snare a bird.[1]

The penalties were severe: 'Joseph Burge, 29, a labourer, 1 year's Hard Labour for being in the night on enclosed land with nets for the purpose of taking. Bruton, 4th Oct. 1876.'[2]

In Dorset the area of Cranborne Chase was a popular one for the poacher. Here the game would most usually be deer. An account dating from the beginning of the last century gives some indication of the nature of the bloody conflicts that took place between the poachers and the keepers of the Cranborne estate.

> I should give some account of the very serious affrays, and bloody conflicts, which have passed there [Cranborne] attended by some murders. But to bare relating such matters is so disagreeable and distressing an office, that I wish to decline it . . . had not a most atrocious action and bloody event recently taken place.
> . . . It is believed, by tradition only, without any authentic

record, that a very bloody engagement once took place between the keepers and the deer stealers, in which several lives were lost, in a part of the Chase in the Parish of Tarrant Gunville ... the spot where the engagement is supposed to have taken place was a gate leading onto a wood, which gate to this time bears the name 'Bloody Shard', and the wood within it that of Bloody-way Coppice.[3]

'Shard' means a gap in an enclosure, particularly in a hedge or bank, and folklore tells that a hand now haunts Bloody Shard Gate, being the hand of a trumpet-major who in 1870 led a gang of poachers who were ambushed by a large group of keepers. The man had his hand cut off in the fight.

The incidents were serious ones and gave rise to civil disorders. However, the traditions usually reduce the blood-letting to a minimum, though the theme of guilt often obtrudes. In one story an informant told of how he went poaching with a few friends. It was a very still night, with no wind, and they wondered whether they would in fact bother to go, as their scent would linger. But as soon as they entered the wood a very strong wind arose and blew the trees about; they became very frightened and ran away. Fifty yards from the wood the night remained utterly still.

A more structured and more traditional series of stories tell of sheep-stealers being accused or encouraged by wild animals, particularly owls. Usually a sheep-stealer goes out and takes a sheep, and an owl in a nearby tree hoots 'Take two, take two'. In another version the bird becomes a pigeon, and while it starts with the 'Take two' piece, it develops into a sadder and more realistic conclusion with, 'Rope, r-r-rope! Hang the man.' In some versions the theme of retribution is even more marked. The poacher or sheep-stealer, having taken two animals usually at the suggestion of the owl, slings them round his neck, one at each end of a rope. He sits down to rest, sometimes at a wayside cross. He falls asleep, and his heavy load slips off the resting place, and suspended in mid-air strangles him.

A happier story, and claiming to be true, was collected from the Blackdown Hills, Somerset.

Old Rab Jennings used to steal sheep, and he used to take them and hide them in a barrel. The police used to search his buildings, but they never found anything. After their search he used to ask them to have a drink of cider, out of the same barrel as he had hidden the sheep in. Though he was later caught, his long period of non-detection was due to the fact that the barrel had a false head. The sheep was in one part, and the cider in the bottom half. Thus the cider could be drawn off, preventing any chance of the 'cider' barrel appearing to be the hiding place for a dead sheep.

The Blackdowns are well known for their traditions concerning sheep-stealers.

### B.2.iii. Highwaymen

If oral tradition expressed a certain sympathy for the poacher, this was not extended to highwaymen. These were outside the social pale, and stories dwelt on their bravado and cruelty on the exposed, lonely stretches of road where they operated; isolated inns became their haunts, and horror—albeit spiced with romance—surrounded their doings. Certainly the roads were not safe places in centuries gone by. As Margaret Preston wrote to her husband from Norfolk in 1500, concerning the transfer of some money:

> The week XX^ti marks she hath delyvered to me in golde for you to have at your company home, for she dare not aventure her money to be brought up to London for feere of robbyng; for it is seide heere that there goothe many thefys betwyx this and London.[4]

Fielding's *Joseph Andrews* gives a vivid impression of what the roads must have been like for travellers in a later century.

The range of hills known as Windwhistle in south Somerset is well known for its grandeur, its isolation and its stories about highwaymen. It is crossed by the busy A30, and has been used as a main coach route from London to the south-west for centuries. The road rises to over 700ft, and is enclosed by an avenue of beech trees. It is exposed and wild in winter. The traditions of the area probably rest to some extent on the activities of highwaymen, or more simply robbers, in years gone by. It should perhaps be noted that the term 'highwayman' as used in so many stories of oral tradition has a good deal more emotive appeal than 'robber'. The traditions extend beyond stories of the act of stealing. Much booty it seems must have been hidden in areas nearby, and it is still to be found. The pub at Windwhistle still has the rings in the wall to which the highwaymen were supposed to have tied their horses. After a hold-up and a murder the highwaymen would throw the body into the nearest field, and the labourers would discover it later in the year when harvesting. A fuller version of the last tradition is given as follows:

In the olden days they used to stop for refreshment at the pub on Windwhistle. The people who they thought had money would go in there, and never come out again alive. A packman went in there one day, and he had his suspicions, and the landlord thought that he would leave his baggage there, but he picked it up and left as fast as he could. The pub had a latch door leading down to the cellar, and they would lead them down to the cellar and do them in, and take their money. Then they would put the man they had done in across the horse, and a man would ride the horse, and ride it on down a little way, and throw the body in a pit. If anyone else working class was going that way the landlord would say, 'Have you met anyone on the road?'

'Yes,' they'd say.

'On a horse?' the landlord would ask. 'Did he have anything?'

'Yes.'

'What did it look like?'

'It looked like they had a pig across 'em.'

And that was the dead man.

Sometimes retribution follows the action of the highwayman. One unfortunate robber on Windwhistle held up a coach to steal money, grasping the window frame with his hand; an occupant in the coach had a hatchet and brought it down swiftly on the fingers of the highwayman, who left behind several fingers and made his escape as best he could. This theme of the severed fingers finds parallels particularly in modern folk-lore—once again with the element of retribution involved.

> A man had gone to Liverpool to watch his own team play foot-ball. The match was against another side, but they were not from Liverpool either. On leaving the ground and starting to drive away from the ground in his car, he was mobbed by a gang of youths, supporting the rival team. They rocked his car, and tried to lift it off the ground. The car was a VW 'Beetle'. He drove off quickly and did not stop until he reached home, when he went to the back of the car to inspect the damage. Inside the grille, above the engine, he found the severed fingers of one of his assailants.

Another story remarkably similar runs as follows:

> A man was driving across Dartmoor one night and slowed down to pick up a hitch hiker, but several more appeared out of the ditch, so he speeded up and they took a swing at him with sticks and other weapons. Next morning he found a piece of bike chain with two fingers attached hanging on his bumper.

The informant added that he had heard several stories of this sort; in some the driver of the car finds the fingers soon after the attack and goes to the police who then inquire at the hospitals in the area to try to find the owner of them.

The theme of an unjustified attack being followed by a some-what bloodthirsty retribution is strikingly familiar. In fact, as with many modern stories that are 'told for true', the tradition at first seems plausible, but on closer investigation is absurd. The width of the grille above the engine of the car in the first tale is not sufficient to allow the entry of fingers of normal size.

Retribution is also a theme in a story from Sedgemoor. Tom Pocock was a famous highwayman who operated in this region and owed his success to the fact that after a robbery he hid in a rhine, empty except for a few inches of water. His hiding place was secure, since even dogs were not able to follow his trail. However, the story goes that he made the mistake of telling his secret and finally he was betrayed. After he had held up a coach and hidden himself, his betrayer opened the sluice gates above the rhine and drowned him. His ghost haunts the moors to this day.

Dick Turpin, one of the most infamous highwaymen, is supposed to have visited the south of England—though whether he actually did so is impossible to say with certainty. While he comes in for his fair share of romantic comment, he was in fact a most undesirable character. 'A surly, sordid robber, pitted with smallpox, whose Black Bess is as legendary as his ride to York. As far as history can show he only visited York once, when he was escorted there to be hanged in 1739.'[5] However, he is said to have visited South Petherton:

> Turpin came to South Petherton one Sunday, when all the people were in church. He came to one of the big houses, the Manor House. He went into the house, and threatened the old lady who was inside, demanding money and valuables. He frightened the old lady and said, 'Now I suppose, when I'm gone, you'll pull this bell and warn all the villagers. I don't know whether I ought not to blow your brains out now.' She begged for her life, because he wasn't too particular who he killed, and he rode off. No sooner had he ridden out of the village than she pulled the old bell, and roused the villagers from the church, and they set off after him. They say that he came up the road to Lopen Head, and then went across a ploughed field, taking one of the deep cut roads down towards Lopen with a jump, and so threw off the people from South Petherton. He then made his way up on to Windwhistle, and so back to London. That was the time when Richard Turpin actually came to Somerset and robbed this place at South Petherton.

The tradition includes the same notion of Turpin's almost supernatural powers as a horseman. There are many deep-cut roads in the area, some of them over 12ft in depth, and the distance from one field to another over this would be considerable.

### B.2.iv. Piracy

The sea coast of Dorset provides one tradition concerning piracy. It also sheds light on the foundation of the Chesil Beach.

There was a buccaneer who, back in the 1400s or 1500s, was chased by the king's ships, and he put in at Abbotsbury, on a very rough night. The next morning the beach had been washed up, leaving him on the inside, and the king's ships on the outside. There used to be a church, or a churchyard up on Golden Cap, and he used to keep his swag in one of the vaults. He did escape from Abbotsbury.

The church concerned is to be found in the parish of Stanton St Gabriel (OS Sheet 177, GR 402924). The chapel of St Gabriel was formerly the chapel of Whitechurch Canonicorum, dating from the fourteenth century, though the chancel is of a later date. The new church was built in 1841.[6]

### B.7. *Trades and occupations*
The various traditional trades and occupations have given rise to their own folklore. The sexton had a lore by which he practised his trade, and he kept the details of the manner of burial of certain 'undesirable' characters a secret. The baker would not make bread in thundery weather, or it would not rise. The cider-maker should not make cider on 19 May, St Dunstan's Day. Just why this tradition has been recorded in the south-west, and what St Dunstan has to do with cider, seems unexplained. However, St Dunstan was born at Glastonbury, and traditions tell that he was a worker in gold and other metals. He is the patron saint of goldsmiths. It is said that he was once tempted by the Devil, while working at his smithy. The saint, realising that it was the Devil, caught him by the nose with a pair of red-hot pinchers and would not release him until he promised to tempt him no more.

Some traditions found in Wessex refer to the now forgotten importation of seaweed to inland areas for use on the land as fertiliser. Stories grew up at Wadeford, near Chard, that the seaweed was brought up by smugglers, and was used by a local factory-owner to put in the tobacco that he was processing. Such traditions of deprecation are widespread and may be heard of almost any product, the most common being 'there's more water in . . . beer, than there is in the river . . .'

A story from Shapwick (pronounced 'Shabic') in Dorset also told of the seaweed used as a fertiliser. It is one of those stories told to show the stupidity of inhabitants of villages other than your own. 1788237

> Once a rather dim lad was working out in the field, unloading a cart that had just returned from the seaside, where it had been loaded up with a fine quantity of seaweed. Suddenly the lad dropped his pitchfork in alarm, for there crawling amongst the tangle of weed was a strange and most terrifying monster. He rushed off in alarm to warn his friends. They returned with him as fast as they could to wonder at the monster that had been found in the seaweed, the like of which had never been seen before. However a man from a neighbouring village, who happened to be passing, took one look at the monster and, laughing at their ignorance, told them that it was what more intelligent people called a crab. Soon the story spread, and the 'Shapwick monster' became a joke in the neighbourhood, pointing to the stupidity of the inhabitants of Shapwick.

The cap of the local cricket team still bears the sign of the crab.

This resembles a story from Aldborne in Wiltshire. Here the natives were remarkable for their slowness and ignorance.

> Years ago a very strange bird landed on the village pond. All looked at it, and it was so strange and peculiar that the village elder was fetched. He was brought in the wheelbarrow, and wheeled round the pond until he had inspected the bird, and at last he pronounced that it was a 'dab chick'. Ever since the people have been called by that name.

This tradition is not as complete as the one from Shapwick, though Wiltshire natives are remembered elsewhere for their slow wits—the 'moonraker' phrase is supposed to have originated there, but this will be dealt with later.

# CHAPTER 3

# COMMUNICATION AND TRADE

### C.1. Roads, paths or tracks

Communication between rural areas of scattered settlement has caused a body of lore to develop concerning roads and bridges. Some of these stories deal with the attempts of people to make the roads safer. It was believed that the sacrifice of a dog, particularly a black dog, beneath the foundation of a road would cause it to stand as a safe passageway for ever. Many of the 'black dog' myths (p 126) may stem from this practice or belief. It has been recorded in oral tradition that the black dog of Blandford Bridge, Dorset, refers to the sacrifice of a dog beneath the bridge foundations. Frazer tells us that 'in modern Greece, when the foundation of a new building is being laid, it is the custom to kill a cock, a ram, or a lamb, and to let its blood flow on the foundation-stone, under which the animal is after-

wards buried. The object of the sacrifice is to give strength and stability to the building.'[1]

In Somerset it is recorded that old buildings will look for a lizard or similar animal when building a wall or suchlike, and burying the animal beneath the foundations will claim that the wall will then stand for ever. On the Blackdowns, the old road-menders believed that the flints that they used to break to mend the tracks had hearts: if you broke open a large flint stone, you would find a heart inside it.

The Fosse Way is prominent in Wessex tradition, both in history and legend. One tradition tells that the Fosse Way was used by pilgrims travelling from the south coast to Walsingham. The road was called Fisher Way, as people used to bring fish along the road from the coast. This tale contains a strange mixture of fact and fantasy. No doubt in years gone by the Fosse Way was an important line of communication, as it still is in places. Certainly the true Fosse Way started at 'the tidal inlet near Axmouth',[2] though by connection it ran down to Honiton and Exeter. It crossed the Windwhistle Hills, from where the above tradition was collected, and on through Dinnington where the first noticeable alignment takes place. It eventually ran through Bath, Cirencester and on to Lincoln. Pilgrims or other travellers may have landed at Axmouth and used the Fosse Way, since Axmouth was, until the end of the seventeenth century, a port of some size. Pilgrims certainly did use part of the Fosse Way according to Latimer who was once rector of West Kington in Wiltshire. He wrote:

> I dwell within half a mile of the Fosse Way, and you would wonder to see how they come by flocks out of the west country to many images, but chiefly to the blood of Hailes.

The abbey at Hales was famous for possessing a portion of Christ's blood.

### C.1.iv. *Journeys*

Traditions of a more local type often tell of the journeys undertaken by particular characters. Often the incidents take place at night, and are sometimes the result of fooling or too much cider. Many of the tales are no doubt based on fact, but have become somewhat distorted and dramatised in the telling. Such stories may have only local importance and significance, being told perhaps about a local personality, familiar to the audience concerned. Most frequently they point to a weakness in a person, or to the fact that he was made to look ridiculous. The anecdotes of a group dressing up in sheets to frighten another fall into this category. One such story told of some lads who went out to frighten an elderly man who was courting and often walked back late across a deserted heath. The lads thought he was rather too old for that sort of thing, and waylaid him in the agreed manner. However, he was not as stupid as they had thought, and since the heath was provided with a plentiful supply of large rough flints, and he was a good shot, he was able to draw some very human cries of pain from the 'ghosts' as they ran off.

The theme of the ghost that was not really there is common. Sometimes of course the attempt to frighten is successful. One informant from the Bristol area explained why his brother had pure white hair, although he was of no great age. Once, long ago when he had been a choirboy, his friends had dressed up as ghosts and frightened him in the vestry. He had nearly died of shock, and as a result his hair had gone white. In unsophisticated times when people held ghosts in more reverence than they do today much sport could obviously be had from these and similar foolings, though no doubt they could result in suffering. A bold informant from Somerset however liked to tell how he was never fooled. The churchyard through which he often had to pass late at night on his way home was said by his elders to be haunted, and if he ever heard or saw anything there he was to run as fast as he could. One night, very late, he was passing through the churchyard when he heard a loud noise, and saw a dark frightening shape. He stood his ground and found neither devil nor ghost but a donkey, which he mounted and rode halfway home—to show to all that he had no fear.

Such stories in their various forms suit the technique of the story-teller, and therefore are to be found quite widely in oral tradition. In more exact forms their appeal rests on the anti-climax following the explanation of the nature of the ghosts. The bathos represents some of the exhibited art of the story-teller.

Two men were walking towards Ilminster, and had taken a short cut over the top of Wake Hill, across Mr Bragg's fields. When they got to the top of the hill, where it was very dark, they heard someone breathing. It was pitch dark. One of them said, 'Who's there?' There was no answer. He said, 'If you don't answer, I'll bring my stick down across you.'

But it turned out to be a donkey.

The location was well known locally for being haunted, and thus the tale assumed additional dramatic force in the telling. Such tales also serve to illustrate the stupidity of popular belief in hauntings, as they tend to imply that all other supposed meetings with ghosts probably had a rational explanation.

A man was walking back late one night, and passed the church as the clock struck midnight. By the church gates he saw the figure of a man. He thought that it must be the ghost of a man who was supposed to have shot himself, and who was supposed to appear at that spot. He ran off frightened out of his wits. It was in fact another man on his way home.

This tale lacks the bathos of the last, and rests on the mistaken identity of a real man, whose supposed supernatural origins inspire fear. This theme is found strongly represented in the following tale from Hinton St George:

There was a story about a black dog that was supposed to be seen at certain times of the year in the village. One night, just after the war, they had been talking about this to an old chap. After, he went down to post a letter. The black dog was also supposed to rattle chains. Well, this fellow went to the post, and he heard a dog ,and the chains rattling. He ran all the way back. It just so happened that a farmer had tied up a dog with a chain near the spot—but the story of the black dog was there all the same.

Dogs with chains and donkeys that have escaped recur in these tales. Others explain why someone came to get lost—such as those of fairies deliberately leading a traveller astray. These form another branch of tradition that will be considered later, for being 'pixy led' was a recognised hazard of making one's way homeward late on dark nights. However, the intervention of supernatural animals, rather similar to a group of stories referred to in the section dealing with poaching, can be mentioned here:

> Old Charlie Boyer went out and got tight, and couldn't find his way home. Going through Staple Park an owl hooted, 'Hooo, hoooo?'
> Charlie replied, 'Charlie Boyer, hay-maker, tatie-digger, wants to go to Whitford Sir, honest a man as ever broke bread.' But all the owl replied was, 'Hooo, hoooo.'

A similar story is told in the Dorset village of Houghton, near Blandford Forum. The inhabitants were known as the 'Houghton owls'. W. Sherren in *Wessex of Romance* (1908), p 12, explains why:

> Many years ago John Joyce, a native of the place, missed his way in the wood, and being both timid and benighted, he called out lustily for help. The only answer to his cries was the hoot of the owls (Whoo-whoo-whoo) mistaken by him for an answering human voice.

For a similar story, perhaps from this source, see Thomas Hardy's *Far From the Madding Crowd* (Chapter 8).

### C.5. Fairs, actual; markets

Most towns and many villages had their own fairs and markets on a scale unknown today. One of the famous Wessex fairs was the one held at Sherborne on the first Monday after the feast of St Michael, known as Pack Monday Fair. Traditions associated with this rather strange name are still to be found, though the fair is now only a memory in the minds of the older generation. In its most simple form the tradition runs as follows:

There was once an old fair at Sherborne, called Pack Monday Fair. It was so called because the workers had a kind of strike, and packed up, thus it was called Pack Monday Fair.

Another explanation runs thus:

It is ushered in by the ringing of the great bell at 4.00am, and by the boys and the young men perambulating the streets with cow horns at a still earlier hour to the no small annoyance of the less wakeful neighbours. . . . It is commonly known as Pack Monday Fair, and there is a tradition that Abbot Peter Ramsam and his workmen completed the nave of the abbey on that day in 1490, and that the name was derived from the workmen packing up their tools. These fairs are chiefly for cattles, horses and sheep. At the last woollen clothes and all sorts of commodities are sold.[3]

Udal, in *Dorsetshire Folklore* (p 130), tells us a similar tradition about the fair's origin.

The tradition collected from contemporary oral sources bears some resemblance to the original, quoted in full. The cause of the workmen packing up their tools had been forgotten, and the excuse for a celebration at the completion of the nave of the abbey lost. Also lost is the sense of enjoyment and merry-making that figures so strongly in contemporary accounts. The old custom of horn-blowing seems to have been stamped out by the police, though in 1884 on the night of 12 October a 'whole body of about 300 assembled at the Antelope hotel' . . . and at 12 o'clock, 'moved off in no particular order and marched once all over the town . . . keeping up an incessant din the whole time with horns, bugles and all sorts of tin trays, that would make a noise. About 2.00am the town is allowed to go to sleep.'[4]

The tradition about the foundation of the fair may have had some connection with the completion of the nave, though it stands more firmly as a piece of folk etymology. A more authoritative explanation of the word 'pack' is of course that of the *pack*-man—pack, 'a bundle of things enclosed in a wrapping or tied together compactly, spec. a bundle of goods carried by a pedlar'.[5]

A market of a very different sort is commemorated in Bristol. Here there is a lane called 'Pitch and Pay', and local tradition has it that during the Plague farmers from outlying areas who wished to sell their produce, but were naturally unwilling to enter the city, would pitch their vegetables and eggs and other commodities at this spot and withdraw. The Plague-smitten inhabitants of Bristol then came and helped themselves, leaving the money for the farmers to collect later.

The tradition is to be found in many other places, though often the traders took the additional precaution of having the coins placed in a basin or dish holding water or vinegar. In 1627 Salisbury market was transferred to Wilton because of the Plague, and there is a stone between West Harnham and Netherhampton where the inhabitants of Salisbury left their money in a basin of vinegar, and the traders from the market at Wilton left their food. The stones on Dartmoor known as the Merivale Rows are also known as the Plague Market, because when Tavistock was suffering from the Plague in 1625 the traders left their provisions there and the townspeople collected them, leaving the money in bowls of water.[6]

Fairs and markets naturally constituted an important part in the trading life of the farmer in Wessex, and they were important social events. Taunton Market today remains rich in chatter and tradition, and Bridgwater Fair still breeds its own traditions. The markets are well reflected in oral tradition.

# CHAPTER 4

# THE COMMUNITY

## D.6. The family

The family as a unit has naturally produced its own traditions. These often seem to tell of disagreements and misunderstandings. Sometimes stories tell of the murder of one brother by another, and indeed this is as old as history; the story of Cain and Abel shows a family dividing, and the inevitable murder. In Wessex, stories of family feuds are often the result of some domestic dispute, or of divided loyalties in the Civil War or at the time of the Monmouth rebellion. Occasionally a brother will oppose the courting of his sister by a social inferior. Such a story comes from Cricket Cross, below Windwhistle. The daughter of a rich local landowner was being courted by the son of a farm worker, much her social inferior. He came over the hills to meet his love at Cricket Cross—a crossroads above the village of Cricket Malherbie. The girl's brother discovered the meeting and was very angry. He came out one night and attacked the lover, slew him, and buried him at the crossroads. His ghost can still be seen there. This theme is common enough to have appeared in literary form more than once. About 1590 Kyd used a similar story in his *Spanish Tragedy*, and many years later Keats used the theme in his narrative poem *Isabella*, which itself was based on a much older story from Boccaccio's *Decameron*.

While the subject of the family tends to occur with some frequency in tradition, the family itself perpetuates those traditions. Stories are often heard from a father or mother, grandfather or grandmother, kept and regarded with almost casual concern as part of common knowledge, but worthy of passing on in time to the next generation—not as instruction, but as things that every well-brought-up person knows.

### D.8. Church stories and legends of its religion

The following section covers a large body of tradition concerning churches. The church for long provided a focal point in the structure of village life, as well as representing a spiritual force that surprisingly seldom seemed to conflict directly with folklore. Christianity and the pagan gods have coexisted with ease, and many traditions that surround the church or the churchyard are pagan in origin. Men have worshipped in one shrine or another for hundreds if not thousands of years, and Christianity came on the scene as the successor to other beliefs that are still strongly maintained through folklore and oral tradition.

Many stories deal with the notion that a church has been moved from one site to another. They usually serve to explain why a church is far from the village it serves, or why a church has been built at one location and later knocked down or destroyed, another local church usurping its functions. The striking fact that emerged in this survey was that these stories were always to be heard where circumstances were right—wherever an isolated or ruined church was found, there was also a wealth of stories to explain it. Nor were these stories confined to the area of immediate study. Consider this tale from Checkendon, Oxfordshire:

They wanted to build a church at Checkendon, and one group of villagers wanted to build it at a place now known as the 'Devil's Churchyard'. This was an old quarry, surrounded by yew trees. However, as soon as they started to build the church, another group of villagers removed the stones at night and built the church where they wanted it situated. The latter group won the dispute, and the church is now where they placed it. The former group believed that it was the Devil who had removed their stones. [Informant: Mrs P. Taylor, Checkendon.]

Often elements of local rivalry are apparent in these tales. A group of stories was collected from Allowenshay, near Ilminster, the site of some church remains (not now visible). Tradition tells that when the building of a church was started there, the monks took the stones away to build the church at Kingstone. Who or what the 'monks' represent, other than perhaps an authoritative ecclesiastical power, is not made clear, but the villagers obviously resented losing their own church, and having to suffer the inconvenience of walking to Kingstone.

A very similar story is told of the parish of West Dowlish, not many miles distant. Here, however, the claim that the loss of the church was due to the deliberate actions of a rival party is not so strongly maintained.

The church was burnt down, and there was a rumour that some of the stones were carried off to Dowlish [East] and rebuilt—but the informant did not know if this was true.

A fuller and more specific explanation is given by the following:

They never built another church at West Dowlish. The story is that they tried to, but what they built by day was knocked down by night. They tried many times, but they gave up. The explanation was that the parish people of Dowlish did not want a church, because if there were two in the same parish, and there were before the fire, it meant paying more tithes. It was the people of Dowlish [East] who went over to knock down the church.

Notice that it is the people of the other village, ie, Dowlish Wake, who are said to have come over and knocked the church down, although the people of the immediate locality (West Dowlish) would have gained as much had the tithes been reduced. Whatever the reason, the people of the parish of West Dowlish must now go to Dowlish Wake to worship, though there is a graveyard at West Dowlish by the ruins of the old church, and a service is still held there annually.

It is worth establishing something of the history of this particular church at West Dowlish, because it presents a good example of how age of a tradition can be discovered. Presumably these traditions have been current since a little time after the destruction of the church. There is some local evidence that the church was burnt down: some charred worked stone was found in a local building, during renovation, which could well have come from the old church. The church in 1535 was valued at £31 7s 6d.[1] In a case heard in Chancery Court in 1692 about rating matters it was stated that there had been neither church nor parochial officers for 'time out of mind' nor 'within the memory of man'. The church was thus destroyed sometime between 1535 and 1600. Its font is still to be seen at East Dowlish. Even if we take the latter date, the stories about the church at West Dowlish have been in circulation for nearly four hundred years.

The tales collected from this place show however a development noticeable elsewhere. The important details are usually that the knocking down is done at night, and the building by day, that the destruction is not done by neighbouring villages, or even for that matter by people at all, but by ghosts, fairies, pixies, druids or 'people who move at night'. The typical story runs like this:

> After the church was burnt down, what they built by day was carried back to Dowlish by night. The informant supposed that the fairies must have carried it back. The informant got the story from an old man who must have died fifteen to twenty years ago.

Altogether twenty-five traditions were collected concerning this location. Each one showed some particular stage in the development of the story. The churchyard naturally enough becomes haunted, and thus cursed, and as a result it is now impossible to build there.

Then people would say that it was haunted, and that you could never build there. All sorts of things were supposed to have been seen there. At certain times of the year, towards the end of summer, things are seen in the old churchyard.

One strange tradition recorded that as fast as people tried to rebuild the church it came down. A voice said, 'Build thy church where a sow and seven young ones are.' This could be compared with the tradition of Braunton Church, Devon, where one of the roof-bosses over the font commemorates the tradition that St Brannock was directed by a vision to build his church where he found a sow and her young.[2]

A further example of the pig being associated with the rebuilding of a church is to be found in Bett, *English Legends* (1952), p 79, which includes a collection of 'changed site' stories from all over England. The pig was responsible for the removal of the stones:

The parish church at Winnick in Lancashire stands on the spot where St Oswald, the King of Northumbria, was slain. It had been intended to build it in another place, and one day's work had been done. But that night a pig was seen taking up the stones one by one in his mouth, and carrying them to the place where St Oswald died. There is a pig sculptured on the tower of the church.

Bett gives another story concerning Godby Cross near Burnley, where the same thing was reported but this time with several pigs.

As the story developed, the notion that the rebuilding at West Dowlish was not only taboo but impossible spread to the stones found round the area of the churchyard. One informant remembered taking a stone from the place and being strongly reproached by her grandmother and ordered to take it straight back. In any case, it was claimed, stones removed from that churchyard would return there of their own accord. Thus the stones have developed a life and existence of their own; this accords with traditions told of standing stones or Drake's cannon ball, and the stones used for the erection of a Christian edifice have acquired through oral tradition the marks and reputations once reserved for stones associated with pagan worship many centuries before.

Within these traditions are to be found slight variations of the building theme frustrated by a supernatural agency. R. Hunt provides a story from Towednack in Cornwall about a church with a peculiarly squat tower:

> The devil came every night and carried off the pinnacles and battlements. Again and again the work was renewed during the day, and as often it was removed during the night, until at length the builders gave up the work in despair.[3]

The tales concerned with the position of a church in relation to the rest of the village that it serves are more truly aetiological, in that they explain in folklore terms something otherwise inexplicable—the true historical reason is probably lost. It is worthy of note that these stories are usually about a church, and a changed-site story about a secular building is rare. The inference would seem to be more than the fact that the church is usually the oldest building in the village, though no doubt its great importance to the whole community added attraction to its acceptance into oral tradition.

The church at Broadway, Somerset, a good example of this group, lies over a mile from the village, alone and isolated. There is no evidence that it was originally surrounded by the village, but perhaps because of the Black Death, or the Plague, the village may have been abandoned and rebuilt some distance away from an original site. The church could have been the only substantial stone structure and been left where it was. Historical evidence is lacking, but it seems more likely that it was during the Black Death period rather than the Plague that this could have happened. There is no visible sign of habitation round the church, and by the time of the Plague some houses of stone structure would have been built and would probably not have been abandoned for good. Holcombe (Mendips) is traditionally a Plague village, and the church there is not set away from the rest of the village.

The absence of historical facts merely illustrates the facility with which oral tradition can provide an answer to a puzzle, to the satisfaction and the entertainment of the people. At this particular location a number of traditions were collected, many of them showing similarity in detail to the other church-site stories considered in this section.

> The story is that the church used to be built where the Con- gregational Chapel now is. However, as fast as they built it the Druids carried it away by night—to where it now stands. They built the church up in the village, but what they built by day, the pixies carried away during the night, and that is why the church is where it is now.

Perhaps the most charming ran as follows:

> They were going to build the church down there in John Baker's yard. What they brought up by day the fairies carried away by night. The informant's father told him that they came in one night and the fairies were carrying away the stones. One fairy was saying, 'I twit', and 'Thee twit', and the old fellow said, 'Ah, the Devil twit the twitting of thee.'

A similar but more general tradition was collected about Curry Mallet church; the church is, however, only a short distance from the main village.

*D.10.i. Courts, trials and methods of proving guilty*
A well-known folklore method of finding a murderer was based on the belief that the corpse would bleed at the murderer's touch. A story collected in several places[4] tells of the murder by Master Babb of a widow who lived near Taunton. She refused him, and much annoyed he hid in her brew-house. He was refused again, and having been hit by the widow with a pewter candlestick he attacked her with a knife and killed her with sixteen stab wounds, leaving the knife in her hands to imply suicide.

Mr Warre, a magistrate at Hestercombe House near Taunton,

D

believed in the old tradition and had the corpse disinterred. The locals from three miles around had to assemble and pass the corpse. As Master Babb's turn drew closer he became afraid, and eventually he lost his nerve and ran away. Troubled by a bad conscience, he eventually gave himself up. The Somerset Assize for 1613 was held at Chard, and Master Babb was tried and hanged in the same year near Wambrook. The contemporary account from which we learn this story is to be found in C.R.B. Barrett's *Somersetshire* (1894), p 218; the notion of the bleeding corpse is not confined to oral tradition, also being found in the Child ballads.[5]

The story of Jack White's Gibbet, Castle Cary, illustrates the same theme; this tale is well-known in Somerset. Jack White murdered a traveller, who had been foolish enough to boast that he carried money, at the crossroads. The corpse was carried to the town, and all gathered round to identify the man, including White who did not want to draw attention to himself by being absent. As soon as White stood before the corpse it started to bleed, and all realised that he was the murderer. He was hanged by the crossroads, which he now haunts.[6]

*D.10.ii. Punishments*
The severity of the penal code in days gone by has left its impression on oral tradition. Some of the tales recorded have become humorous or light-hearted versions of incidents that in themselves must have been quite serious.

> Back in the time when you could be hanged for debt there was a man who got himself into trouble this way and was to be hanged for debt. Somehow he managed to escape, but to convince the authorities of his death and to evade the hanging he filled his coffin with stones, and had a funeral service. The coffin full of bricks was buried. Later he was seen alive and well, and was called 'Resurrection Johnny'. His name was John Grabham.

Sometimes a particular place has been noted for the site of an execution or hanging. This sometimes simply adds a name:

Gallows Hill, on Bere Heath, Dorset, or Gibbet's Brow, Mendips. On the A31 between Wimborne and Bere Regis is Red Post, traditionally the location of a gibbet. The signpost is still coloured red to commemorate the fact. The tradition has added local importance, since it is said that the Tolpuddle Martyrs were hanged there. This is typical of the way oral tradition alters facts to fabricate its own story, carrying events of local importance: the six farm workers convicted in 1834 of joining an unlawful trade union were transported for seven years, not hanged, William IV granting them a free pardon in 1836.

Okeford Fitzpaine, Dorset, retains the door of the old village lock-up, still there, preserved in a wall in the centre of the village, all that is now left of this old form of punishment and retained as a piece of village history, not to be sold. The story goes that the last person to be held in the lock-up was made to drink cider through a straw through the iron grating in the door, and as a result became very drunk. Okeford Fitzpaine was well known for its cider-making and its orchards.

Cider has caused the downfall of many, among them, the story goes, the late Cardinal Wolsey, who came to Somerset when still a young priest, being instituted as vicar and schoolmaster at Limington, near Ilchester, on 10 October 1500, when aged twenty-nine. Tradition has it that he went to the fair at Lopen, enjoyed the cider too much, and as a result of his subsequent disorderly behaviour was put in the stocks by the first Sir Amais Paulett. When Wolsey became lord chancellor years later, it is said he had his own back on Paulett by summoning him to London and compelling him to live in the Middle Temple for five or six years. The stories collected varied in detail; some have it that it was the stocks at Martock, while others say it was those at Ilchester. Whether the story is true or not is another matter, but it appealed to the tellers in the first place because it brought a mighty man, not of their planet, down to a level they could comprehend. Part of the appeal, that of a cider-sodden Wolsey being clapped in the stocks to sober up, retains to this day an element of the delightful.

Punishment can sometimes involve lovers who because of their feelings acted in a particular way that was not thought proper by their superior. Muchelney Abbey produces one such story:

> A long time ago there was a monk at Muchelney Abbey who had a secret relationship with a nun. The sin was discovered and as a penalty they were both walled up alive. The place can still be seen at the top of the only existing stairway. The monk now haunts the building.

This version was collected in about 1928, though the story is still told locally. In 1968, however, it had lost much detail. The custodian of the place said quite simply that he had heard a story about a monk and his 'girl friend' but he did not know that the place was haunted. Such a story comes obviously from a long tradition—it may be an addition to an older story—and also from the fact that there is a doorway at the top of a stairway that has been bricked up. The door motif is similar to that told of Donyatt Church (Chapter 1, A.2.i), and hints of the same idea are frequently found elsewhere in oral tradition. Manor Farm, Dowlish Wake, has a tradition that a lover was walled up dead in a tunnel, which was sealed over, but this is now only vaguely remembered. The story from Muchelney shows a loss of detail in transmission, though it has provided the theme for romanticised versions found elsewhere. R. Tongue in *Somerset Folklore* has it as 'the heart-breaking tale of ill-starred lovers', stating that a similar story is told of the Old Abbey House, Barnwell, Cambridge. Boger[7] tells the story of Muchelney and quotes a poem by Dean Alford of Canterbury concerning the incident. The poem must be the final version of the story ever to be told:

> An abbot, who in medieval times was married in secret to a fair lady, were rudely parted at the altar, and he was hurried senseless to the abbey. In time he rose to be abbot.

The rest of the story is told in the poem, a work of considerable length and doubtful poesy. A 'holy lady' came to the abbey at night and asked to see the abbot. She came from St Mary's

Priory, near the abbey, and she took the abbot back there. The lady turned out to be his former wife, and they returned to the abbey. After 'long hours have flown, to wedded rapture given', he hid her in the tower, where she died soon after; he followed suit, undoubtedly full of grief. There was a local tradition that a large house on the other side of the Parrott, half a mile from the abbey, was a nunnery and that an underground passage ran between the two.

That it made good subject matter for a poem has boosted the tradition with a certain importance. But this version does not belong to the same genre as the oral tradition current today, and the comment about the monk's 'girl friend' is probably far nearer the truth than any heart-rending account of ill-starred lovers. The foundation of the abbey is variously attributed to Athelstan in AD 939 as a penance for having his brother killed on false evidence, or as a thank-offering after the battle of Brunanburgh in AD 937. Others ascribe it to King Ina. It was a fine building by all accounts, and rich, holding large quantities of land throughout the region. The story probably dates from before the abbey was taken by Henry VIII, on 3 January 1538, a time when it seems that it did not have a very good name. The king's commissioners reported that, 'he found the abbot negligent and of doubtful character, and ten brethren which was ignorant and unlernyd'.[8] The monastery seems to have suffered from a relaxation in the rules which allowed 'strangers and women' and even 'imprudent girls' to come into the cloister garth.[9] Bishop Ralph, who visited many religious houses in an attempt to restore a sense of morality and good conduct, came to Muchelney in 1315, 1328 and 1330. It may be that the tradition dates from this time, or from a similar period of notorious behaviour among the monks there.

By way of direct comparison to this story there is a tale from Tisbury, Wiltshire. Place Farm was once owned by the abbess of Shaftesbury. Fair Nell, a very beautiful nun who lived there, committed the sin of looking upon a man. As a punishment she was condemned to walk for ever in a tunnel that (supposedly) connects Place Farm with the top of Ridge, where today is a copse known as Farnell's Copse (ie Fair Nell's Copse). Presumably she is still walking.

This theme of the walling up alive of a guilty party is a very old one, going back at least to Greek times. Antigone was to be walled up alive for giving her brother burial rites. The tradition rests on the idea that it is the supernatural agency that causes death, not the human persecutors themselves. It is not hard to imagine the degree of consolation that this thought must have brought the victims.

*D.10.iv. Stories about crime, including murder*
We have already seen how crimes in general, and murder in particular, have caught the imagination of the folk, and so become expressed in oral tradition. Murder itself is always dealt with in a sombre way, and the stories that centre on the theme are ubiquitous. Murder was probably no more common in times gone by than it is today, but its total hostility to human life has linked it in the folk memory with all that is evil and dark, however these feelings may be labelled. St Michael's Hill near Montacute is supposed to be haunted by the ghost of a woman who was killed by her husband, himself a worthy of Montacute. The development of oral tradition becomes more interesting when we can read a first-hand account of the actual incident, and then compare it with the traditions collected. Just this may be attempted with the murder of Samuel Churchill on 4 March 1879, at Knowle St Giles, Somerset. The facts display something of the primitive nature of life at this time. The account is to be found in the *Western Gazette*, Friday, 7 March 1879, under the heading of, 'Alleged murder at Knowle St Giles'. The house where the murder took place was occupied by the victim, a labourer aged eighty-three, his wife Charlotte, fifty years old, and her mother, 'who is an imbecile, who is upwards of ninety years of age, and is bed-ridden'. The account continues:

> On Tuesday morning last, about ½ past 8 a woman named Elizabeth Whatley . . . was carrying some tea to her husband who was working in a field besides the Churchill's house. As she was passing by the back of the cottage she heard cries of

'Murder'. She at once proceeded to a gap in the hedge and looked through.

She saw the cottage and swore that she could see a woman inside pushing something towards the fireplace. She heard groans. Her husband, on being told, did nothing, as he said the Churchills were always fighting. Then 'she heard the key turn'. Three-quarters of an hour later, Mrs Churchill was seen to leave the cottage and walk in the direction of Chard. She called at the Ship Inn, and at 10.30 returned to her cottage at Knowle. Her son Samuel, aged about twenty-one, was walking near the cottage, and she asked him if he wanted anything to eat, but he said no. She then called out to George Whatley, the man who was working in the field near the cottage, and said that Samuel had fallen into the fire, and was badly burnt.

> On entering the cottage a horrible spectacle met his view. In the old-fashioned chimney corner lay the charred remains of Samuel Churchill. The fire was burning slowly, and in fact it was almost out. The upper part of the body of Churchill was resting on the smouldering embers.

A doctor and the police were sent for. Superintendent Gerity 'discovered marks of blood on the settle, on the table, and on the floor near the fireplace. He also found a bill-hook under the chair, on which there ware signs of blood.' She was arrested and taken to Ilminster, where she was charged. She was tried at Taunton, and the account of the trial is to be found in the *Western Gazette*, Friday, 9 May 1879. In this account she is called Kitty.

> Tried on 5 May 1879. Guilty and sentenced to be hanged by the neck until she be dead, and her body buried within the precincts of the prison where confined. To be executed at 8.00am on the day of May instant.[10]

The paper confuses one or two points. Her name seems to have been Catherine or Kitty, rather than Charlotte as first stated. The family relationships seem strange, though the paper does say that they were ill-thought-of locally. The couple were supposed to have cohabited for twenty-five years, and been married for only nine. He had a daughter by his first marriage to whom he had left all his money, while Kitty wanted it left to her only son also by a previous marriage. The paper does not go into where the ninety-year-old imbecile comes in, but one can see the elements of oral tradition at the first stages.

Certainly the story is remembered in one form or another over a fairly wide area. The stories did however display many of the usual features of transmission. A few examples will demonstrate this.

> There used to be a woman who killed her husband with a bill-hook in the spring time. The man was called Samuel Churchill, and this was his second wife. She killed him and came up to the Ship Inn to a little shop that was there then. She put his body on the fire, and went off shopping. Of course only a portion of him was burnt, and someone looked over the hedge, and saw what was left of the body and reported it. She was arrested and hanged at Taunton—the last person to be hanged there. She was buried at Taunton where the murderers were usually buried—in High Street. There is now a road made over the place. This was seventy to eighty years ago, and the informant remembered his parents talking about it.

For a story told nearly a hundred years after the event this version shows remarkable accuracy; it is probably only second-hand. It even has the date of the event correct—'in the spring time'. It has however acquired the 'first and last' motif, and the way the informant told the incident of the first discovery of the body makes it sound as if the body was placed on a bonfire outside the cottage. The accuracy is far from typical.

> There was a woman, Kitty Churchill, who pushed her husband on the fire and murdered him. The informant thought that this must have been the first person to be convicted of murder, though he was not sure of this.

Here the theme of the 'first and the last' has become attached to something else. In the third example the name is changed, the relationship between murdered and murderer is altered, and the 'first and last motif' varies yet again:

A woman the informant thought was called Nama Rayes burnt her father on the fire, and she was the last to be hanged publicly at Taunton. The murder was done by pushing him on the fire and burning him.

Other versions gave variations in fact. One said that she was hanged at Exeter gaol, another that it was the son who had committed the murder, but that it was Kitty who had taken the blame for it. The final twist associates the murder and murderer with a local crossroads, mentioned before, where Mary Hunt was supposed to have been buried. Then the murderer was finally buried at the crossroads, or sometimes even assumes the name of Mary Hunt. So a local crossroads grave that in some sense has become redundant—in that no local tradition can explain its existence—is perhaps in the process of acquiring a *raison d'être* from an historical event that would explain its supposed corpse quite happily. The other notable development of the story is that the cottage where the murder is reputed to have taken place now has the ghost, in the fireplace, of course, of the murdered man. In fact it is doubtful whether the cottage is still standing.

This is a good example of a documented event that has passed quite naturally into folklore, and by being retold for nearly a hundred years has developed many variations, typical in themselves of the processes of oral tradition.

CHAPTER
5

# HUMAN LIFE

*E.3. Individual characteristics*

A tradition still lingers in parts of Somerset that people with red hair are witches. This belief is in fact closely linked with a more general tradition about the nature of red hair. Pixies were characteristically red-headed, but 'The Danes were hurdyeaded men who beat Ow's'.[1] There seems to have been a definite dislike of red-heads on the Quantocks. They have been called 'Danes' bastards' through the centuries. Even today a very old person may call a red-headed boy a 'proper little Dane'. It was even considered wise to lock up red-headed people on New Year's Eve: this was the time when witches were supposed to be most in evidence, and therefore were most dangerous. In fact this last tradition rests on the confusion of dates arising from the superimposition of the Christian calendar on the Celtic. According to the latter, witches were supposed to travel abroad on Hallowe'en night, as this was New Year's Eve. The obvious modern equivalent would be 31 December.

As with many traditions the complicated and not altogether logical lore extant today is the result of the mixture of several different factors. First there is the idea that red hair is associated with the Danes, who certainly penetrated into parts of Wessex. The Danes may well have sometimes been characterised by their hair, though the tradition goes back a good deal farther than this, and it seems that the Danes inherited a prejudice established before their incursions. Red-haired people have for centuries had a reputation for being deceitful and unreliable, not to mention the fact that they are supposed to have short tempers, 'probably owing to the tradition that Judas Iscariot had red hair'.[2] The folklorist, A. H. Krappe, quoting a German proverb against red hair, adds: 'It stands to reason that the aversion did not arise among Irish or Jewish people. The adage reflects merely the feeling of the ordinary Teuton when he faced his Celtic neighbour and enemy or the Jewish tradesman who inhabited the ghetto of his cities.'[3] It is interesting that while the modern prejudice against red hair has lost many of its old forms, it hangs on with surprising tenacity. Its perpetuation in modern folklore takes a rather different form.

Extant in oral tradition today is the idea that red-headed girls have a physical abnormality of the vaginal passage, this taking the form of some sort of tooth. (Another modern tradition concerning hair tells of a woman with hair piled high on her head in a large beehive. Inside this hair-do is a maggot that is slowly eating its way into her head. In this case, however, the hair does not have to be red.)

Stories on a lighter note tell of the man with a great beard. The one collected and told below must be typical of many incidents actual or supposed where the cruel trick of cutting off half a beard is executed.

> There was a story about a man who had a great big beard. He was very proud of this great beard, and in fact he more or less worshipped it. One night the man and his friends spent the evening in the pub, and a good deal of drinking was done. In

fact the old man with the beard got rather tight, and finally fell asleep. His fellows then cut off one side of his beard while he slept. He woke up and was very cross, but it was too late to save his beard.

### E.6.i. Strength

Many stories still told of men in days gone by who had prodigious strength may well have had some factual foundation. This tale is told of the inn on Windwhistle:

> Back in the olden days they had a very fierce dog at the pub. There used to be a small passage through the pub to the main bar. The landlord offered £50 to anyone who could finish the dog. A sailor went in there one night and the dog chased him up the passage, and he killed the dog with his bare hands.

Strength can be made to show superiority. One informant, himself an old man, told a story that he regarded as true, and that had been told in his family for at least three generations. His grandfather had been taunted by some men from Merriott, became angry, set about the men and single-handed 'knocked them all sky high'. Merriott men were always regarded as foreigners and even today a true Merriott inhabitant regards outsiders with suspicion. Merriott is a dialect island, different in many ways from the area around it. W. G. W. Watson in his book *Somerset Life and Character* discusses some of the details of this (pp 98ff).

### E.10.viii. Manner of burial

Burial rites have figured largely in oral tradition, as they were, and to some extent still are, regarded as most important rituals, which will affect life beyond the grave. While there are stories to be told about actual deaths, there are many more about what happens to the corpse after death. One story from Somerset tells how the corpse was being transported for burial when it was carelessly dropped, and the skull of the body smashed on the ground and split open. This allowed the ghost of the deceased to escape, and the ghost has haunted the spot since that time.

The funeral rites require special observances, and though the tradition of the Wake has long since ceased to be remembered in Wessex, other beliefs linger. If you kiss the face of a corpse you will not dream of the body, and the same tradition is told in other places, only there you are meant to touch the dead person. A person will have difficulty in dying if the bed has pigeon or partridge feathers in it. If the corpse does not become stiff it means that it is waiting for another member of the family to join it.

Burial was also most important. It was said that a corpse should always be buried with the feet towards the east, though if the person was a clergyman then the feet should be to the west. This was so that on the Day of Judgement, laymen would stand up facing the east, from whence the day would dawn, but clergymen would be facing the other way, ready to speak to their congregations.

Not all traditions of death are so light-hearted. The corpse had to be treated with great respect; wrong procedure could result in years of trouble from a ghost. The north side of the churchyard was reserved for the poor, the unbaptised and sometimes the suicides, so corpses buried there were likely to be troublesome: if a dog was first buried in the area this would lessen the chances of hauntings. The sexton could bury the corpse upside down if he thought that the person had been particularly wicked, though a stake through the heart was the usually accepted way of keeping a corpse firmly in the grave. The yew trees found so widely in churchyards today once had their practical uses. Collinson in his *History of Somerset* writes the following:

> Our forefathers were particularly careful in preserving this funeral tree, whose branches it was said were used for mourners to carry in solemn procession to the grave and afterwards to deposit therein under the bodies of their departing friends. The branches thus cut off from their native stock, which was to shoot forth again at the return of spring, were beautifully emblematical of the resurrection of the body, as, by reason of their perpetual verdure, they were of the immortality of the soul.

By Collinson's time (1791) this tree, which originally had pagan associations, had become fully incorporated into the Christian rituals.

An interesting burial is told of a man called Ettricke who lived at Wimborne Minster, Dorset. He was a squire and a magistrate, and apparently said 'When I die I do not want to be buried below ground, above ground, inside the minster, or outside the minster.' So he was entombed in the wall. Anthony Ettricke is a well-known figure in Dorset local history. He was the magistrate who tried Monmouth, and he was also a successful trader. According to Hutchings he was 'very humoursome, phlegmatic and credulous'. He remained persuaded that he would die in the year 1691—a mystical date in the calendar because it reads the same either way up. He therefore had his tomb made and the date cut on it. In fact he died in 1703, and the date had to be changed, as is evident from the inscription on the existing coffin today.

Popular tradition tells us that he would not be buried inside or outside the church because he had a disagreement with the people of Wimborne. However, he left £1 in his will for the church of Wimborne, and for bread for the people of Wimborne. An account of Ettricke is to be found in Aubrey's *Brief Lives of Contemporaries* (vol 2, p 18). The coffin is still to be seen in Wimborne Minster, at ground level, set in the wall, so that it does comply with the wishes of the deceased—although in fact it does not contain his remains! A traveller on 13 September 1750 wrote:

> The tombe of Mr Etrick which is made like a stone coffin half in the wall and half in the church which was made in his life time, this being his fancy . . . but his relations put him in a vault underground directly under the tomb.[4]

When the minster was restored in the years 1855–7 his remains were found beneath the coffin in a moist state, and they were carefully replaced where they were found. Details of this restoration are to be found in the *Salisbury Journal*, 3 October 1857.

The theme in tradition is quite a common one. The motif is often that of a person who cheats the devil of his soul, sold previously to contract and agreement that burial should not be in a church. Hutchings (vol 4, p 423) mentions a part of an old tomb that used to touch the outer wall of the Minterne aisle of Batcombe Church, Dorset. The village legend told that it covered the grave of 'Conjuring Minterne', who vowed that he would be buried neither in the church nor out of it.

Udal tells us of a corpse that was laid out in the village of Lulworth with a penny in one hand and a little wooden hammer in the other. Whatever the original purpose of the hammer, the penny seems an obvious provision for a journey into the other life. Another tale from Charborough Park includes burial with a hammer, though in this case the hammer's purpose is clear: the corpse wanted to be able to hack his way out of his coffin in case he was buried alive by accident. This was something that people used to fear, as the diagnosis of death could be faulty. Old people used to insist that their relatives should stick pins in them after they had died to ensure that they were really dead, whereas in a small village near Mahon in Minorca the corpse is left for a time with the coffin open at the cemetery, near the bell-rope, so that if it revives it can ring the bell.

Squire Holnest of Charborough made even more elaborate preparations.

> One of the Squires of Charborough was called Holnest. When he was getting old he began to worry that his family would not give him a proper burial. He thus had a coffin made and his men whom he employed were summoned to be his bearers. Every time he felt a slight twinge, or thought that his end was near, this old man would get these men to carry him in his coffin, as though he were dead, around the park. When any of them got out of step or jolted him, he would 'come back from the dead' and shout at them. When he did finally die, he was buried with the old equivalent of a hammer and chisel, and a bottle of spirit. The top of the coffin was made of glass. All this was so that if he did wake up, and he was not dead, he would be able to hack his way out of his coffin.
>
> The story goes that his coffin was later found to have a hole in

the top, and that no animals would go near the path that had
been taken when the bearers had practised the funeral.

### E.10.xi. Grave-robbing and robbers

From the time when it was believed that the dead one had to
go on a journey, it has been the custom to bury with the corpse
certain objects that would be useful in that journey. Even up to
comparatively modern times it has seemed right to bury jewel-
lery and other precious objects with the deceased. This custom
has of course led to grave-robbery, a crime looked upon as
serious, not only because it disturbs the dead, but because the
objects sought properly belong to the dead person and—to a
superstitious man—might carry something of the grave with
them that could be transmitted to the thief. So many of the
stories found in oral tradition concerning grave-robbers contain
a strong element of retribution. Rings are the items most often
concerned; often they were not removed at death, partly because they were considered to be an integral part of the deceased,
and partly for the simple reason that a ring that has been worn
for decades is difficult to remove. At its most simple the tradition
runs like this:

> The informant had heard from an old relation that there was
> a woman dug up at Lambrook, and her rings were stolen from
> her.

Hutton, in *Highways and Byways in Somerset* (p 276), gives us a
very similar story, only with a little more detail:

> There is a legend of a lady who was buried in a trance at
> Seavington St Michael, and was wakened by the sexton, who
> would have stolen her rings.

In oral tradition however the story finds more complete expres-
sion. The informant told this story about the Church of St
Decuman, Watchet:

> There is in the church the tomb of a young woman. She was
> buried with all her jewellery. Thieves came soon after the funeral
> and took all the loose jewellery, having broken into the tomb.

They further cut off that which was tight about her fingers and wrist. The circulation started up in the corpse again, and she is supposed to have got up and walked out of the church.

No doubt sometimes these stories stood as warnings to the unscrupulous. Certainly the one of St Decuman's Church is found in other versions. Poole[5] tells us that the corpse in question was that of the mother of Sir John Wyndham 'who being supposed dead, was buried alive in the vaults of St Decuman's'. Fortunately for the woman, the sexton heard some noise and investigated it; finding it came from the coffin, he opened it, and found the lady alive. Whether there is any truth in this story or not, the important point is that the story got about, and became suitable material for a robbing tradition. Thus the good lady is buried with her jewels, and revived on being cut on the finger, no doubt in an attempt hurriedly to remove a tight ring.

The blood-curdling effect that the 'resurrection' of the corpse quite naturally would have on the robbers is shown by a dramatic story from Russia, which has the same theme as its basis. A schoolmaster fell in with a group of robbers who forced him to help them rob the tomb of a rich woman recently buried in the crypt of the church. He went down and opened the coffin and was ordered by the robbers to take off the seven rings on the corpse's fingers. The first six he managed well enough, but the seventh would not come off, as the finger was curled up. The robbers instructed him to cut off the finger. No sooner had he done this than the corpse awoke, and cried to her 'brothers and sisters' in the crypt to arise and help her, as she had had no peace in her lifetime and now it seemed she was to have no peace in death. The dead rose up in one accord and chased the schoolmaster from the crypt. He took refuge in the choir, but the dead contrived to pile their coffins one on top of the other to reach him; he repelled them with a long pole until the clock struck midnight, when the ghosts returned to their places in the crypt. The schoolmaster was found more dead than alive next day. He confessed to the priest what had happened, and died soon after.[6]

## E.12. Suicides

Murder lingers long in folk memory and stories about murders pass easily into oral tradition. But the material is not as plentiful as that supplied by suicides. For one murder in the area of south Somerset covered in detail, there were nine stories about different suicides. Murders and suicides arouse, however, the same feeling of sinister unnaturalness, and the same paraphernalia accompanies the tradition that becomes established after such events; an uncanny reputation is attached to the location of the death, making people unwilling to be near the place after dark, and it is believed that the ghost of the dead person will haunt the spot. Action to prevent the ghost from walking has been discussed before, but a suicide was not allowed a Christian burial in the churchyard, except that a lucky corpse might find a place on the north side of the church.

Traditions of suicides seem likely to be based on some degree of fact, and indeed these traditions often contain no more than the details of the event. It is at a more sophisticated level that they do show some of the traits of narrative, as will be seen. The authenticity of the stories is more or less impossible to check, as suicides' names would not appear on burial registers, and early coroners' reports for the area in question were destroyed.[7] Folklore is mainly concerned with successful suicides concerning which, for obvious reason, there is no court evidence. Thus the traditions take their place as part-fiction, part-fact, in the ever-developing oral tradition perpetuated in a small community either out of morbid interest, or because it offers the explanation for the unnatural reputation that some place has acquired.

At its most simple the tradition is found in this form:

A man named . . . in the farm house at Ludney killed himself, probably because he had problems. The informant knew of no ghost or anything like that.

A similar brief story, without any explanation for the despair, adds the beginning of the haunting theme:

There was a pond nearby where someone committed suicide. The place afterwards had a bad reputation, but was not considered to be haunted.

The tradition develops to its full extent in another story collected a few miles away:

> There is a copse at the top of Holmoor Farm, where a man hanged himself. There is supposed to be a ghost there.

Or:

> Someone was supposed to have hanged themselves in the old mill, and their ghost now haunts the old building.

Such traditions are simple and show a natural development, without accretions. The next example is much fuller, and contains the curse motif, resultant from the suicide:

> So and so down . . . in Ilminster, her father hanged himself in the house at Dowlish, the other side of the farm house. They say that if the spot where he hanged himself fell down they would never be able to rebuild it again, because he hanged himself there. He said to the cowman, to give the cows some mangolds, and he'd go on, and when the cowman came back he saw the man hanging there.

A really good story-teller can take the facts and work them into a memorable tradition. Thus in the final example the oral tradition of a suicide has become far more than a simple memory or explanation; it is an entertainment, albeit somewhat macabre:

> The Spekes who held all the property lived at Jordans. One of the young Spekes and his wife held the living at Dowlish Wake. Before this, but not very long before, the wife died. He went to preach in the church as usual. The last hymn he gave out was number 19 in *Ancient and Modern*, 'The ancient morn hath passed away, and spent too soon her golden store, the shadows of departing day creep on once more.' His text was, 'And I put my body under, and put it into subjection, lest after I have preached to others I myself might be cast away.' He did not take the trouble to walk down the steps from the pulpit, but he jumped down and tore off his surplice, and went up to Wake Hill and committed suicide. His wife had died before he took the service.

Other versions of the same story had it that he killed himself by throwing himself into the cesspit, his wife having died in childbirth. The tradition of Speke's suicide is interesting for a number of reasons. The location has a bad reputation in any case, and the suicide adds to a ghostly tradition that has existed from early times.[8] B. Speke was inducted in 1857, and was succeeded by F. M. Mules in 1881, that year being the last of Speke's incumbency. It is reasonable to suppose that he died in that year, so the tradition is ninety years old. Speke's last child was born in 1878 or 1879, which would seem to upset the theory that the death of his wife in childbirth was responsible for his suicide, unless the child was stillborn. Speke was fifty-one when he died.[9] The text quoted by the informant as being Speke's sermon text is found in 1 Corinthians ix, 27, 'But I keep under my body, and bring it into subjection; lest that by any means, when I have preached to others, I myself should be cast away.' The hymn however is not to be found as number 19 in *Hymns Ancient and Modern*, or anywhere else in that hymn book, but is found at number 940 in *The Methodist Hymn Book*, the first line reading 'The *radiant* morn hath passed away.'[10]

# CHAPTER
# 6

# NATURE

A rural society lives and works with nature, and to some extent at least its economy depends upon nature. The casual observance or the specific incident has therefore passed through the folk mind into oral tradition. Stories about nature are often very localised, having immediate significance only to an audience familiar with locations mentioned. On a wider scale however these stories are of more general interest. While named locations seemingly limit the acceptance of a story generally, the same motifs recur in different forms; a story told of one place can in fact be virtually the same story as is told many miles away. This trait in the story of oral tradition is by now obvious from this collection alone. The first group of traditions to be considered in this chapter illustrates the point well.

*F.8.iii. Lakes*
The unknown, strange underwater world presented enough

material for the imaginative mind to contrive stories. Lakes and pools in isolated positions add even more potential, and a series of traditions has developed around them. No doubt many of the beliefs associated with inland waters stem from the time when our Celtic predecessors believed in and worshipped the spirits dwelling in them.

First is the belief that certain areas of water contain monsters, or are the homes of unnatural objects. Loch Ness, well out of this area, is the classic example; a body of oral tradition surrounds the claims of those who believe the monster exists. In the survey area, a tradition was collected about the reservoir at Chaffcombe, near Chard. The informant said that he had been returning late at night, and he and his friends had seen some sort of a water snake in the lake. The tale was told with some wonder, and shows the almost instinctive belief in supernatural monsters of the deep. Sometimes however it may not be animals that haunt the deeps of lakes and ponds. Grendel and Grendel's mother in *Beowulf* are finally destroyed by the hero in their cavern under the mere. Dozmary Pool, on Bodmin Moor, is by tradition the pool from which Arthur received the sword Excalibur, and while the Lady of the Lake has not the evil generally attributed to Grendel, she is nevertheless an underwater supernatural creature. Dozmary Pool, now glared at for months of the year by trippers briefly extruded from coaches, has lost some of its mystery, but isolated, windswept in winter, it still has some of its old primeval character.

The notion that lakes and pools are bottomless is widespread. It often arises where a horse or waggon has accidentally fallen into the water and has not been seen again. The mystery inherent in a dark and probably relatively deep pool is heightened by the tradition that it leads somehow to the depths of the earth. Consider the following stories:

> There was a deep pond down the road, into which a waggon and horses disappeared, and nothing was ever seen of them again. It is called Maul Pit, and it is supposed to be bottomless —that is what the informant was always told when he was a child. The informant mentioned that in his opinion he was told

this to stop him playing dangerously near the pool when he was a child.

The informant had heard of Maul Pit, and he had heard that there was a certain pit in the area that was supposed to be bottomless, but he was not sure if it was Maul Pit.

The rationalisations of the first informant may well have some truth in them. Maul Pit is probably an old 'marl pit', marl being a clay soil mixed with carbonate of lime and used as a fertiliser, and so the pit was probably man-made. A large pool in the River Parrett at South Petherton was supposed to be bottomless, and again some vehicle was supposed to have plunged into it. An old pit full of water at Trent Barrow near Sherborne is so deep that no one has been able to measure its depth and is called a bottomless pit; a coach and horses was supposed to have plunged into it and never to have been seen again. A pool in the River Stour at Durweston has a similar story: I have not heard it said that this one is bottomless, but a horse and cart once bolted, it is said, ran into the pool and were never seen again. An example outside Wessex is in one of the caves at Castleton, Derbyshire, which is supposed to contain a bottomless pit; indeed the pit is claimed by the owners as a chief attraction for visitors to the caves.

*F.8.viii. Caves*

This section and the next, F.8.x, contain some of the traditions that for one reason or another have particularly caught the imagination of man. To the folk mind it is not the obvious cave formations, those resulting from the nature of the rock and particularly from attrition by sea or rivers, that are the material for traditions. Many of the cave stories concern the unlikely places where the bedrock is unsuitable for the natural formation of caves, and where artificial construction would be expensive and unlikely. It all adds up to a desire for mystery, to narrate a story about a secret that only the select few know and even fewer have actually seen. Similarly any material that would contribute to the growth of a cave tradition is easily assimilated.

The following tradition collected in Somerset illustrates this well:

> The informant said that there were caves under Cricket Court, and that during the Monmouth rebellion soldiers hid there.

This house has extensive cellars. Somehow the Monmouth rebellion notion has been added to this fact, possibly because the house was used to billet soldiers during World War II. A linked tradition collected nearby told of a 'dungeon' that went from one side of the hill to the other. This 'dungeon' was a small building marked by a door set in a wall by the roadside, and housed the water supply for Cricket Court. The door was for obvious reasons kept locked; thus, to the people who regularly pass it and wonder what it really is, it becomes a dungeon, and by extension an evil place, until we end up with the version given by one informant:

> We never liked to pass by there, and we were told that the reason why it was always kept locked was because the Devil had been shut in there. We used to call it 'The Devil's Dungeon'. It certainly had a strange reputation, 'It used to make you feel—well, I don't think I'll go along there.'

A second informant gave a slightly different version:

> There was a water dungeon out by Cricket Malherbie, known always as 'The Devil's Dungeon'. It was called 'The Devil's Dungeon' because if there was wrong committed, then the Devil was in there. Someone was murdered, and the body was thrown in there, and it has been kept locked ever since. She had never seen it unlocked.

Both versions of this story illustrate the way in which the desire for mystery and a sense of hidden secrets help to evolve a tradition.

### F.8.x. Underground passages

Many of the comments about traditions concerning caves apply equally to those concerning underground passages. The difference lies in the ubiquitous nature of the underground passage tradition: it is indeed hard to explain why quite so many old buildings should be credited by tradition with tunnels, passages and other subterranean communications. Grinsel called these tunnel stories, 'perhaps the most valueless of all traditions'.[1] Indeed, if you look to folklore to provide an indication of some now-forgotten fact, tunnel lore will be disappointing. The obsession with tunnels must have its origins in something other than fact.

In an area of south Somerset of about 100 square miles, sixty-three different stories were collected. In Dorset there were nearly as many stories about tunnels as about ghosts. The length of the supposed tunnels varied from a few yards to several miles, the only thing the traditions had in common being the fact that the reputed tunnels in nearly every case were believed to run to and from old buildings; in only a couple of cases were they reported to surface in the middle of a field. Sometimes the tunnels were directly associated with a particular activity, smuggling being a natural favourite:

> There is a tunnel running from Sturminster Castle to the mill, which was used in the days when smuggling was a flourishing industry in Dorset. Barrels of brandy were stored there after being carried up the river Stour. The tunnel is said to have been made by the inhabitants of the castle during the middle ages, who were in constant fear of attack. They therefore constructed the tunnel from the castle to the mill from whence they could escape by boat.

References to smuggling and Sturminster Castle are vague. Sturminster was certainly on the smuggling route from West Lulworth, and nearby Fiddleford Farm was once a depot for contraband.[2] However, Hutchings in his *History of Dorset* (3rd edn, vol I, p 339) states that the castle or manor house was partly pulled down in 1732, and the remainder in 1840, so Sturminster Castle was probably in ruins when smuggling was at its height. The River Stour was never navigable for any distance, no more than it is now.

Monks and nuns have also been associated with various secret passages:

> There is a tunnel from Houghton Church that leads in the direction of the old tithe barn at Winterborne Clenston, and in the

other direction to Milton Abbey, at Milton Abbas. This tunnel was used by the monks who lived at Milton Abbey. Another tunnel runs from the abbey to a big farm house called Quarleston Farm, and another from the abbey to Delcombe Manor.

Altogether this would involve seven and a half miles of passage. At Wool, Dorset, there is a tradition of a tunnel from Wellbridge Manor House to Bindon Abbey. At Cudworth, Somerset, a passage connects Knight's House Farm with the church. 'This dates from the time when the monks lived there.' Hinton Priory is supposed to be connected with Clergy House, Crewkerne, by a passage; this is a distance of three miles. There is a report of a tunnel from Forde Abbey to Hay Farm, where there was also a priest hole, so the priests could escape down the tunnel and hide in the farm. Next in popularity comes the tradition that the tunnel is from the Manor House to the nearby church. The distances involved in these traditions are more realistic. The first example continues the nuns theme:

> There was supposed to be a passageway that ran from the dining room of the Manor House, Whitestaunton, to the family pew in the church. The entrance of this passage was supposed to have been located in the church by the side of the Brett vaults. This was never followed up. The informant thought that the passage had something to do with the nuns.

At Dowlish Wake there was supposed to be a tunnel from the Manor House to the church, and this was also said of Donyatt, though Park Farm was substituted for the Manor House which had been pulled down in 1877. Sometimes tunnels ran from the church to an old barn (Puckington), or from the church to an old cottage (Whitelackington), or even from one old building to another (Wood Court to Ashill Farm). The variations are numerous, but many contain a reference to a church, and all refer to old buildings. One from Dorset told of two humble houses connected by a tunnel:

> There are two old cottages facing each other near the church in Charlton Marshall. One is called Wayside Cottage, and the other has been empty for some time. The informant said that

there was an underground passage that had been discovered, that ran between the two cottages under the road. If you walk across the road, you can feel that it is hollow. There is also a secret room in the empty cottage, and people are not sure if it is a priest's room, or just a secret room.

Tunnels are difficult to maintain and very expensive to dig. Nearly all these tales must be complete fabrications. Yet they occur with almost as much frequency as ghost stories, and are subject to far less scepticism: to an unquestioning mind they are to a degree feasible. They certainly illustrate the large place that mystery and presumed knowledge of the unknown have in the folk imagination.

### F.9. Wells

Wells in folk tradition are usually either 'fairy wells', that is wells with some magic lore associated with them, or more simply curative wells. There are obvious difficulties in classification as some may fulfil both functions in tradition. Further, many wells are now either lost and forgotten, or exploited in some way that renders them almost unrecognisable. The fairy well at the bottom of the tea garden, into which the visitor is requested to throw his coin, seems to have little connection with any traditional wells, though the ritual does stem from observances not altogether absent from folklore today.

One of the famous wells that is still to be seen housed in a comparatively modern stone structure is at Cothelstone, on the Quantocks. This is known as St Agnes's well. It was visited by the 'love-sick' according to tradition, and St Agnes is traditionally the patron of young virgins. Her day is 21 January, and on St Agnes's Eve young virgins were supposed to dream of the man they would marry. Obviously the Cothelstone well is a traditional fertility spring, and Miss Tongue has an interesting story in which the woman who wanted a husband and children visited another well near to St Agnes's well with favourable results, not wishing to trouble the saint, who would probably be taken up with more deserving cases.[3] Often it was thought necessary to leave a coin, usually silver, or even a pin by or in the well. No doubt this is where the notion of dropping the penny in the well and wishing comes from. Sometimes divination resulted from the way that the coin fell. It was lucky if the coin fell flat, though sometimes tradition held that if the coin fell to the left the answer was no, but if it went to the right the wish was granted.[4] The Cothelstone well is also known for its curative properties, especially for its ability to cure sprains.

Another St Agnes well is found at Whitestaunton, in the south of Somerset, near the Devon border. There is a tradition that Queen Henrietta, Charles I's wife, wished for a child here and had her wish granted. Charles married Henrietta Maria in 1625, though it is impossible to say whether the story dates from this time or whether it has been revived much later.[5] Once again the well's fertility powers are prominent, though locally it also has the reputation of being able to cure all sorts of troubles. It is worth a visit, and is found to the north of the house, in waste lands by the remains of what is generally thought to be a Roman villa. Set in a wall, it is reached by a long narrow tunnel passing under the road. Its situation may well point to pagan origins, and possible use as a fertility well, long before Christianity, but until some reliable excavations have been undertaken theories about it have to remain tentative.

Another saint's well is to be found at Watchet, south of St Decuman's Church. This well is somewhat overgrown, but was in its time quite famous. It is supposed to have sprung up after the murder of St Decuman, on the spot where his head fell; some versions have it that the well was used by the saint to wash, and that he bathed his severed head in its water, since which time it was reputed to have magical properties. A number of wells are to be found near churches, and as with St Decuman's well the familiar mixture of pagan and Christian tradition is sometimes present. Stocklinch Ottersey used to have a well supposed to have curative properties thirty yards or so from the church. A well near the church was obviously useful, for baptism and other purposes, and the traditions associated with these wells may point to their use in more primitive times, or more simply to the folk mind working to make a spring both a symbol of life and of mystery. St Mary's well in the crypt of Glastonbury Abbey is a holy well that has retained its religious nature completely. The ritual use of water for baptism may have originated in pagan times. At Cerne Abbas in Dorset is a cold spring in which it was believed new-born children should be dipped, provided it was done with care—that is to say facing the rising sun, the immersion taking place as the sun rose.

Many other wells are associated with cures, though some of these show forms of ritual, not unlike the one mentioned above. At Symondsbury near Bridport in Dorset is a well whose water is said to cure sore eyes; the water must be taken as soon as the sun rises, as the sun's rays touch it. A spring near Walditch in the same area is also supposed to be good for the eyes. Near Merryfield, Somerset, is a spring called by the locals Skivvers well. On May morning, 1 May, those with freckles should go there and take the water at sunrise. Freckles, thought to be a blemish, could also be cured by bathing the face in May dew, before sunrise. Traditions about Skivvers well are still widespread in the area, the well being a place of some importance in its time. Now it is little more than a cattle-hole, surrounded by mud and not easily accessible:

Scivvers well is where the airfield is now. It was a great annual event round the area once. They used to assemble there at some time, and dance all around it, until the water would rise, and flow over the top. It did this because it was boggy ground.

It used to be quite an occasion. They would go there on certain days of the year and drink the water, and it would cure complaints. There might have been some sort of a fair there as well. It was certainly quite an event.

Collinson took special note of the well:

In a field in this parish [Ashill] belonging to the Earl of Egremont, there is a medicinal well, bearing the name of Skipperham well, the water of which is of a singular property, and has thus been analysed.

There follow thirty-two points of analysis, including such comments as:

> It is very cold but never freezes . . . goes off upon keeping . . .
> an infusion of ash bark in this water turned almost instantane-
> ously to a beautiful light green, with a blueish circle at the top
> . . . its uses in medicine have generally been in cases of scor-
> butick eruptions and inflammations of the eye from the same
> cause.[6] A gentleman who lately drank a large quantity found it
> to create nausea and purging.

Collinson concludes that it contains some iron, some sulphur and alkaline salt, and a small quantity of muriatic (hydrochloric) acid:

> It may justly be ranked among the light chalybeats, and which
> require to be used on the spot.[7]

The well is not the only one of its sort in the area, and traditions collected from the area confused one with another. For instance, one or two informants claimed that Wood Court had a well with curative properties, and though this seems unlikely, Wood Court certainly did have an ordinary well. Horne mentions mineral wells at Horton and Dillington; the former is known as Hazel well.[8] There are two springs between Ashill and Wood Court, but these are not chalybeate. Miss Tongue tells of another called Skimmington well at Rock Hill near Curry Rivel. Scivvers well is called Skipperham well on the map. Horne names it as St Cyprian's well, thus implying that it is a holy well, though there is no local tradition to support this. However, he does add that it was spoken of under many names, such as St Nipperham's and Skiverton's, both supposedly being corruptions of St Cyprian.[9] It is also supposed to be a well that ebbs and flows, and bubbling up at certain times of year, and it has been suggested that its popular names are a corruption of some old word implying this. Miss Tongue lists it as a 'danger-ous well. The ebb and flow of this is supposed to foretell national disaster.' She calls it St Nipperton's (Cyprianus).[10] This information does not agree with oral traditions collected in the area about the well, and one would add that her description of Skimmington well has a far closer resemblance to it.

One tradition collected told of a very different sort of well—not dissimilar to the motif discussed earlier of the 'bottomless pit'.

> There was a story about the well that was behind the Windwhistle pub. One day it dried up. The story goes that there was an earthquake in Lisban [*sic*], and the well dried up at exactly the same time as the earthquake, then the water disappeared like cider running through a tunegar.

A tunegar is a dialect word for a funnel.

### F.10. Woods and trees

In some parts of Wessex it is still believed that trees have a life and consciousness of their own. Trees can therefore be agents of good or evil, depending on their nature, and may participate or intervene in the life of man to punish or protect as they think fit. This relic of pagan lore finds its way into oral tradition. The oak was able to take its revenge as it is shown in the story still told of the tree's revenge.[11] Some trees are regarded as good—the ash, the beech, the holly and the apple—and this may have bearing on their original place in the ancient tree-worship rituals. The elder and hawthorn are not thought of very highly, and a widespread belief has it that hawthorn in the house will bring bad luck; I have recorded this belief in Dorset, Wiltshire and Somerset. The disruptions on the bark of the smooth beech, where old growth has ceased, is thought in areas of Dorset to represent the 'evil eye', and the sinister beech grove at dusk is an unlucky place in which to be found alone. Hambledon Hill in Dorset has a dense yew forest that has produced a number of traditions explaining its origin. Generally held to be an unlucky place, some say that it was planted by the druids as a grove in which to worship, others that it was planted by archers in later years to provide a ready supply of wood for their bows.

*F.12. Birds*

Ravens have a long history in folklore, and are generally regarded as unlucky birds, or at least birds that need treating with respect. A brief story about the bird is found in Pimperne, Dorset, which links it with the famous ravens of the Tower of London. The tradition has it that years ago a raven escaped from the tower and flew to Pimperne, where it is to this day, and can sometimes be heard flapping about. The tale adds to the raven a mystical quality that suits its rare appearance in the area.

# CHAPTER 7

# FOLK MEDICINE AND TIME

*G.1. Stories of folk-medicine cures*

While the folklore concerned with medicine and cures in general
is large, there are fewer traditions told about the cures themselves, and these tend to be stories of exceptional instances.
Tales about wart-charming are well known generally, usually
containing the notion that a person had many warts, usually
over fifty, and because of the action of the wart-charmer they
disappeared in a short period. One of the most famous traditions about a cure comes from Bath in the north of the area.

Prince Bladud, the eldest son of the King of England, was
banished from the court because he had leprosy. He went into
the country and became a swineherd. In due time the pigs
caught his disease. Bladud came to Swainswick where the pigs
suddenly moved into a marshy spot and wallowed in the mud.
Bladud took action to remove the swine, but found that the

marsh was in fact warm. The result was that both the pigs and the prince were cured. Bladud was received back into the court, became King of England and built a city by the springs that had cured him.[1]

In folk tradition it was usually the witch who was able to execute the cures, and many of the traditions concerning medicinal cures centre on stories about witchcraft, and will be dealt with under the appropriate heading (J.2.iii).

## H. TIME

This section includes some of the festivals that are associated in oral tradition with particular times of the year. Calendar customs in general, such as wassailing, burning the ashen faggot and the Minehead hobby horse, cannot be examined here, as this book deals with traditions expressed in some form of narrative. However, very many of the traditions do have stories told about them, some explaining their origin. Others that have now ceased to be celebrated are remembered in oral tradition, and are told by the old to the young rather as an oral narrative would be.

### H.1.iii. Midnight
Midnight is an important time in the folk story. Even in the traditional story of Cinderella, midnight is the time when the good spells cease to work as a new day starts. In oral tradition midnight offers a certain dramatic sense to a story, and it is therefore often included regardless of the lore that justifies this inclusion—that ghosts and spirits are more likely to appear at that time. Thus we find traditions like:

> . . . people used to say that between twelve o'clock and one o'clock Mary Hunt would rattle her chains . . .
> . . . Mary Hunt was supposed to appear there at midnight.
> . . . the people believed that at midnight every night his ghost would be seen going through the church gates.
> . . . at twelve o'clock at night you would see a light in the window of the Rectory . . .

Those spirits that are supposed to love darkness and dislike light would naturally choose to appear at the time when light was farthest away. The midnight moment, complete no doubt with doleful church bell, is an element that no good ghost-story-teller would want to omit.

*H.1.v. Dawn, cock-crow, etc*

If midnight is the time when ghosts and spirits are to appear, then it is at cock-crow or dawn that they must vanish. *Hamlet* has it quite clearly: the ghost appears a little after the clock has struck twelve, and disappears again when the cock crows, heralding the dawn. Though the section heading above seems to make dawn and cock-crow synonymous, this is partly the result of a popular misconception: cocks in fact crow well before dawn, and the fact is acknowledged in folklore itself, for instance the belief that when the cock crows at midnight it signifies that there will be a death. Similarly cocks crow during the day, and then, according to folklore, they herald the arrival of a stranger. The association of dawn and cock-crow is only partially based on fact. The Romans divided the day into sixteen parts. The third of these divisions (3.00am) they called 'gallicinium', the time when the cocks began to crow; the next was 'conticinium', when they ceased to crow; the fifth was 'diluculm', dawn.[2] The ballad-writers were much aware of the significance of the cock. Many of the versions of 'Sweet William's Ghost' contain references to the ghost being forced to leave the loved ones because the cock crew. The cock stands as an effective power against spirits of the Other World, quite independent of the association with the dawn. In pagan lore the cock is used to raise the Devil, it being particularly effective if black in colour.

Its use in religious rituals goes back to India, although the Greeks called it a 'Persian bird';[3] in classical mythology the cock was dedicated to Apollo. It was venerated by the Goths who used it as a war ensign.[4] The cock is a symbol of vigilance and still stands on many church towers. Its virtuous nature probably stems from Christianised lore, though it undoubtedly inherited some of its qualities from pagan sources. Much belief here centres on Peter's denial of Christ and the cock crowing three times. Further it is believed that when the cock ceases to crow the Day of Judgement will dawn. Christianity makes the cock 'good' in intention, and its vigilant crowing would naturally frighten a ghost that belonged to a pagan lore. Marcellus says of the ghost in *Hamlet* (1, ii):

> It faded on the crowing of the cock.
> Some say that ever 'gainst that season comes
> Wherein our Saviour's birth is celebrated,
> The bird of dawning singeth all night long;
> And then they say no spirits can walk abroad.

While the cock sings, ghosts cannot walk about. Here it is for this reason alone, and not because of the dawn, that the ghost is excluded.

The lore concerning the cock and dawn is a mixture of various elements. In Wessex there lingers some oral lore representing this mixture. The black cock is regarded with some suspicion, while cock-crow will keep away spirits, and herald the dawn. The colour of the cock remains important (see J.1.iv, p 108).

### H.2. Stories of local festivals

Two villages in south Somerset provide local festivals that have general similarities with customs observed elsewhere, though the details are unique to the places concerned. The festival is called 'Punkie Night'. A punkie is a general term for a mangold, turnip or similar vegetable that has been hollowed out, a face or design cut through the skin, and a candle placed inside. The result, in darkness, with candle lit, is an effective pattern, or usually a grotesque face. Such lanterns are widely made by children, and frequently in association with Hallowe'en when they are used as a novel decoration and occasionally with the idea that they keep away evil spirits.

The custom associated with Hinton St George and Lopen differed from general tradition in the following ways. First, the festival was only associated with these two villages; other areas, while using the punkie as a lantern at Hallowe'en, did not observe the tradition with such interest and festivity. Secondly, the custom is observed on 29 October, and it is claimed that its origin is an incident of local importance, one passed down over the years in oral tradition. Thirdly, each village claims that the other stole the custom from it. The body of tradition concerning the festival was found to be considerable. There follows the result of what was collected, starting first with the traditions from Hinton St George:

> Punkie Night was in early November. The story about it was that years ago the men of Hinton went to Chiselborough Fair, held on the first Wednesday, or some time like that, in November. All these people went to the fair, and coming back at night the fog descended, and they got lost. They went into the fields, and hollowed out mangolds, and set candles in them to provide light to see their way home. The event is remembered each year by the children making these lanterns. It has now become quite an event, a prize being awarded for the best punkie.

> This event takes place on 28 October. The children go into the fields and get mangolds, on which they carve pretty scenes, a mask, a design or something. They hollow them out and put a candle inside, and go round the village for pennies. They sing, or rather chant:
> > It's punkie night tonight
> > It's punkie night tonight.

> Although this festival is observed in other places in England, it is only at Hinton that it is on 28 October, because in the olden days this was the date of the fair down at Lopen and Chinnock. Once the men of the village went down there, and got rather tight, and lost their way in the fields. They carved themselves lanterns to see the way home. Meanwhile the women of the village were hunting for them with scarlet cloaks, and trying to fetch them home.

> The men went to the fair at Chiselborough, and because they were so long coming back their womenfolk and children went out and made lanterns from mangolds to search for the men.

> This custom of Punkie Night was well known. The song however was:

Give us a candle, give us a light,
It's Punkie Night tonight.

The children now beg for money. It had also been started in
other places. It all started on Hallowe'en, when the men went
out to Chiselborough Fair. They got drunk, and were unable to
find their way home. The women went out to look for them,
hollowing out mangolds to make lanterns.

Similar traditions were found concerning Lopen:

Punkie Night was stolen by the Hinton people, although it
originated at Lopen. It all started because the Lopen men went
over to Chiselborough Fair, and got lost on the way back. The
women of Lopen went out to try and find them, lighting mangolds to show the way.

This had been the custom ever since the informant could
remember. The children would go round singing the song,
'It's punkie night tonight', and collect money that they would
share out to buy fireworks. The story of how it originated was
that one night a gang of men went over to Chiselborough Fair,
and it was so dark that they could not see their way home.
They scooped out mangolds, and put candles in them, and that
is how they reckon the custom originated. Variations to mangolds
are vegetable marrows. In Hinton they now give prizes for the
best punkie. The informant knew of no other village that did
this.

The information collected and printed above shows the usual
local variations in details. The use of the punkie has previously
been recorded as taking place at Hinton St George and Long
Sutton,[5] but not at Lopen. The punkie is distinguished by the
ingenuity and complexity of design being greater than is exhibited in the usual mangelwurzel lanterns found elsewhere.

The date and the nature of the custom are made plain by the
above accounts. While 28 or 29 October is claimed as the
authentic Punkie Night, the fourth Thursday in October is now
chosen at Hinton; such standardisation is obviously more con-
venient. At Lopen the custom seems to be less strictly adhered
to, and the date varies, becoming confused with Hallowe'en and

5 November. One informant at Lopen told me that the children used Punkie Night to go round and collect money for fireworks.

At Hinton St George the custom remains an event of local importance. A procession carrying punkies, chanting the song, goes through the streets, and a local person is asked to judge the punkies, a prize being given for the best. Versions of the song collected were only fragments of the one given by Opie, though most of the ideas were present, and I have heard children at Lopen mention the 'Adam and Eve' line. There seemed to be no music remembered, and the lines were chanted. Opie's version runs as follows:

> It's Punkie Night tonight
> It's Punkie Night tonight,
> Give us a candle, give us a light,
> If you don't you'll get a fright.

> It's Punkie Night tonight,
> It's Punkie Night tonight,
> Adam and Eve wouldn't believe,
> It's Punkie Night tonight.[6]

The last line of the first verse was the only one I did not come across, and it seems by its nature to be something of a folk *ad lib*.

The origin of the custom, and its purport, have been something of a mystery. The folk explanation is not without substance, as there was a large fair at Chiselborough held on 29 October, for horses, cattle and toys. Although it is possible that lanterns may have been used by people going to the fair or returning late at night, the intricate workmanship required to make them would hardly have been employed by womenfolk to escort their tardy, and one suspects cider-sodden, husbands home.

In the first place it seems credible to associate these punkies with other mangelwurzel lanterns found elsewhere. They were used to keep evil spirits away at the time of Hallowe'en. 'A girl at Pontypool . . . says that as soon as it is dark on Hallowe'en they take the lighted "Jack-o-Lanterns" and put them on their gate-posts, to "keep evil spirits away"; and this practice of putting turnip lanterns on gate-posts also prevails on Exmoor, and on the Brendon hills in north Somerset.'⁷ I myself have seen such a lantern on a gate-post in Dowlish Wake, not far from Hinton St George, showing people the way to a Hallowe'en party. The punkie designs do look rather like gargoyles, and their design could be thought to frighten evil spirits. Their use in association with Chiselborough Fair, and perhaps an actual incident, started a new branch of the tradition, with its own explanation for the origin of the lanterns.

In the second place, however, we must examine the name punkie, used locally here. One writer quotes an authority as having stated that 'punkie may have come from pumpkie, ie, pumpkin, and really originated from the USA'⁸—a view I think it hard to accept.

Jack-o-Lantern is not unknown in Somerset. This is the 'flame-like phosphorescence flitting over marshy ground (due to spontaneous combustion of gases from decaying vegetable matter) and deluding people attempting to follow it'.⁹ It is of course also known as 'Walking fire', 'Ignis Fatuus', 'Will o' the wisp' and perhaps most significantly of all, 'Spunkies'. In parts of Somerset, Jack-o-Lanterns are called 'Spunkies' and are believed to be the souls of unbaptised children, doomed to wander until Judgement Day. 'Stoke Pero Church is one of the places where "they spunkies do come from all around" to guide this year's ghosts to their funeral service on Hallowe'en.'¹⁰

In Pontypool the mangold lantern is a Jack-o-Lantern; in Somerset it is a punkie. If we associate the two words *punkie* and *spunkie*, we at once associate the two ideas, and a punkie becomes a mixture of the spirit embodied in and portrayed by the lanterns to ward off evil, and a representative of those spirits of death themselves abroad at Hallowe'en.

### H.4.v. Twelfth Night

As a result of the change from the Julian to the Gregorian calendar in 1752 Christmas Eve became Twelfth Night. Christmas Day became Twelfth Day but in the unofficial folk calendar it was still referred to as Old Christmas Day. By the same folk calendar Twelfth Night was called Old Christmas Eve. Certainly there is some case for assuming that the festivities remembered on Old Christmas Day, and still observed in places, are a result of this calendar change—although Twelfth Night was a festival before this time, probably a survival of the old Roman 'Saturnalia'. The festival as remembered in the folk calendar is a time of some importance: it traditionally marks the end of the Christmas period, and is still regarded by some in parts of Somerset and Dorset as the true Christmas Day. One informant near Taunton stated that when he was younger Twelfth Day was always a holiday, much as Christmas was, and while essential work was done, the major part of the day would be devoted to some sporting pastime like rabbiting.

Oral tradition strongly insists on the religious nature of the date, and on the fact that it is the *true* Christmas period of the old calendar. Miss Tongue records the typical tradition concerning the date, the story of a pilgrim who went to Glastonbury from Ilminster and returned with nothing more than a small thorn from the holy thorn. He prayed beside it, and it grew fast. He promised that it would bloom on Christmas Day, but the day came and went and the thorn did not come out into bloom. On Old Christmas Eve however there was a disturbance in the streets, and on looking they saw all the animals from miles around going through the streets in procession to the thorn where they kneeled in front of its white blooms.[11] Miss Tongue gives more detail, though I have not been able to locate the holy thorn in Ilminster, and if there was one there it is now lost from the memory of man.

This was not true for other holy thorns and traditions about Old Christmas Eve collected in the area. Consider the following.

The informant had heard that the cattle were supposed to go down on their knees at midnight, Old Christmas Eve, but he had never seen it.

The informant had heard that it was supposed to be true that the cattle went down on their knees on Old Christmas Eve, but that he had looked, and he knew that it did not happen.

He knew of no holy thorn at Ilminster, but he thought that there was one at Chaffcombe.

Altogether there were four informants who remembered something about a holy thorn at Nimmer, and two who remembered one at Chaffcombe (both places are near Chard). There were also holy thorns at Whitestaunton and West Buckland,[12] but these too have passed out of tradition.

The main holy thorn was the famous one at Glastonbury, and it was from this one that cuttings were supposed to have been taken to generate others. That the tree was reputed to be particularly virile when it came to planting its cuttings no doubt stems from the original story of Joseph of Arimathea. He came to this country after the crucifixion, with the holy grail; he landed at Wirral—called after his weariness, 'Weary all'—and he planted his staff in the ground, where it miraculously sprouted and grew into a thorn. Another version is that he planted his staff and made it sprout to persuade cynical natives of his powers, and that when they saw it they became peaceful and amenable to his cause. The earliest description of the tree is found in Camden.

> I shall be reckon'd among the Credulous of our age, if I speak anything of the Wallnut-tree here [Glastonbury] which never budded before the feast of S Barnabas, and on that very feast day shot out leaves in great abundance; or the Hawthorne-tree, which budded on Christmas-day as if it were in May; and yet (if men may be trusted) those things are affirmed by several credible persons.
>
> The Hawthorne-tree has been cut down these many years; yet there are some still growing in the Country from branches of that; as particular in the garden, where the other stood, and another belonging to an inn there.[13]

The tree once had two trunks, but a zealous puritan cut one down. He would have chopped both down, had he not been 'miraculously stopped by cutting his leg with the axe, and injuring his eyes by the chips flying into them'.[14] Another version has it that the tree was cut down by a puritan soldier, but it was washed down the river where it took root again.[15] The walnut tree noted by Camden shares a tradition similar to the hawthorn's, though it is less well known. Collinson mentions it as growing beside the thorn in the abbey churchyard, and never budding until 'the feast of St Barnabas, viz the eleventh of June'.[16] He tells us that the tree is 'now gone also', and replaced by 'a very fine walnut tree of the common sort'. Of the thorn however he is more specific. He writes that there were once two, but in the time of 'Queen Elizabeth . . . a puritan exterminated one and left the other, which was the size of a common man, and viewed in wonder by strangers'.[17] People even started to export branches of the tree, such was its curiosity value. It was finally cut down in the time of Charles I, 'but other trees from its branches are still growing in many gardens of Glastonbury and in the different nurseries of the Kingdom. It is probable that the monks procured this tree from Palestine, where a great abundance of the same sort grew, and flowered about the same time.'[18]

The present thorn, standing in the grounds of the ruined abbey, cannot be the original, though it may be a cutting from the one the historians mention as being of note in times past. The tradition that Joseph of Arimathea originally brought the thorn here in the form of his staff belongs to a much larger body of belief that includes Joseph's arrival in England with the grail and the foundation by him of the abbey at Glastonbury. The origin of these legends is found in 'a group of apocryphal writings of which the *Evangelium Nicodemi* is the chief; these were worked upon at Glastonbury between the eighth and eleventh centuries'.[19] The happy possession of a thorn of the sort that was likely to bloom around Old Christmas Day added to the virtue of the place, and became sanctified in the folk memory, and in some cases part of their religious belief. The present thorn is as holy as you wish it to be.

Assimilation into oral tradition established the thorn as an object of veneration and pilgrimage. Thus when the calendar was altered, traditions developed concerning Twelfth Night, helped by the significance the date had in any case. The thorn is mentioned in *The Gentleman's Magazine* for the year after the calendar change, 1753. The people of Glastonbury were under some embarrassment as to dates, owing to the changes.

> A vast number of persons attended the noted thorn on Christmas Day, new style, but to their disappointment there were no symptoms of blooming. So they watched it narrowly until 5 January . . . when true to tradition it bloomed once again.[20]

Cuttings of the thorn would have been taken—officially or otherwise—to many parts of the area round Glastonbury, and venerated as holy afterwards. The tradition that the cattle kneel in their stalls on Christmas Eve, or march to the thorn, is an extension of more widespread lore; generally tradition has it that the beasts knelt in their stalls in the stable at Bethlehem. The interesting thing about all these traditions is that they first developed not from some primitive remnant of pagan lore, but from learned or literary sources, and that, through a mixed and complicated set of incidents—the calendar change, the fame of the thorn at Glastonbury—they have become an important and still-remembered part of the folk tradition.

# CHAPTER 8

# POPULAR BELIEF AND PRACTICE

'Popular belief' embodies those generally accepted principles in the folk mentality that were, and in some cases still are, fundamental to a way of thought. This often involves the lore concerning omens and curses, dreams and taboos. The stories that result from this area of belief naturally take a good deal for granted, and usually emphasise the validity of the beliefs rather than their invalidity.

## I.4. Participation and sympathetic magic

Sometimes animals can affect the lives of humans. In a story from Dorset that the informant heard from his father the deer in the park have a particular effect on the lives of the owners of the estate.

A long time ago a German white stag had been brought into the herd of deer that is kept loose in Charborough Park. At this time the squire who lived in Charborough House had been having trouble in producing a son and heir. His wife had so far produced a string of daughters. Meanwhile the white stag had caused the deer of the herd to produce two or three more pure white stags. The squire feared that the herd might become overrun with deer of that sort, so he ordered the fawns to be shot, and also the white stag. His wife became pregnant again, and the squire wondered how he could be sure that he would have a son.

One day some gipsies came to the house, and the squire asked them how they could guarantee that the child would be a son. They replied that if the white stag was killed there would never be any sons. Luckily the white stag had not yet been killed, and there were in fact now seven of them. Sure enough, later that year the squire's wife produced a son, and from then on the white deer were a must in the herd.

Several generations later, another squire had so many sons and no girls that he was forced to shoot all these deer, and later the wife produced the long awaited daughter.

The story is interesting for a number of reasons. The colour of the stag is unusual, and there seems to be a direct link between the success of the white stag herd, and the owners of the land. Notice that the herd had increased to seven in number at the critical time. Seven is a magical number.

In her book, *Forgotten Folk Tales of the English Counties*, Miss Tongue tells of a magical white hart of Kilmersdon (Mendips) that brought joy and fortune to all who saw it. Here the white hind is certainly a fairy animal.

From Bryanston House in Dorset comes another story that links animals with the prosperity of the owners. The Portmans used to keep peacocks in the grounds of the house. It was always said that if the peacocks were to go or be sold, then the Portman family would follow soon after. The 3rd Viscount Portman sold the peacocks shortly before his death, and the house became a school soon afterwards. A similar tradition surrounds the ravens of the Tower of London.

*I.6.i. Dreams*

Dreams have long been regarded with a degree of awe, as giving glimpses into the future. While dreams are common in the Bible and visions have a mystical significance, the dream of prophecy in folklore is more unusual. One tale from Dorset deals simply with a dream:

> It was said that an inhabitant of Blandford Forum once dreamt, before the advent of the railway, that he saw a great monster with fire coming out of its head, running along the ground. It vanished into the ground at the Milldown and in the dream the monster was full of fire and people. It made a loud whistling noise as it went. The dream prophesied the path taken by the railway in later years. The monster was of course a steam engine.

The story is also found in literary tradition, though this version was collected directly from oral tradition. It is hard to establish whether such transmissions have been maintained in true oral tradition, or whether they have received added impetus from print.[1] With the increase in interest in local history and folklore the perpetuation of traditions through a literary source must be reckoned as a growing part of the process of transmutation. The branch of the Somerset & Dorset Railway mentioned in the tradition was started from Wimborne on 13 November 1856 and the line was officially opened in 1863 on 31 August.

*I.6.iii. Predictions*

Dreams are often found in tradition in the form of a prediction or a warning. In a story from Chard, Somerset, however, the dream becomes a vision that conveyed useful information:

> There was a shortage of water in Chard, and an old man called Dwelly saw in a vision a plentiful supply of water above Combe St Nicholas. They dug there, and sure enough there was enough water there. Some of Chard's water does, even now, come from Combe St Nicholas.

The decline of country estates is again considered in a prediction about Hinton Park, Somerset. An informant told the following tale:

He had heard it said many times down there, but he never thought that it would come true. The old saying was that:

Hinton House is a dreary spot,
Hinton House will be forgot,
Here and there a shady tree,
And Hinton House will cease to be.

This has now more or less come true. There are a few trees left in the park, but since the estate has been sold up, the farmers have cut down many of the trees to cultivate the land. In many ways the view from the house is like a desert.

The informant is correct in his comments about the park. The estate has recently been sold up, and the land bought up by farmers who have cut down many of the fine old trees to aid extensive grazing and cultivation.

A prediction is supposed to have been the cause of the building of Brown's Folly, east of Bath. A local dignitary was told that his daughter would die on a certain day. He ordered the tower to be built with a room at the top, and his daughter was placed inside it. Food was sent up in a basket, and on the day she was to die it came down untouched. The girl had died, and further investigation showed that the cause of death had been a snake bite. The snake had somehow managed to get into the basket of food. This story probably occurs in many places. I have also heard it told about the tower of a house near the Sea Walls, Bristol. In this version the snake reached its unfortunate victim in a bundle of firewood, and the prediction was made by a gipsy.

### I.8. Talisman, *efficacious for various things*

The lore dealing with the talisman is extensive but while it is still very much a part of the folk tradition few narratives have been found that have the talisman as a main motif. In general traditions the notion of the talisman retains acceptance in such things as touching wood, crossing fingers, salt thrown over the left shoulder when some has been spilt, and so on. One talisman held to bring luck is still found to a limited extent on the Chesil Bank in Dorset: the Holy Stone, a stone that has a natural hole in it, is esteemed for its virtue. Fishermen used to thread a stone of this sort with a wire, and place it at the bow of their boats before launching out into the bay. This would ensure their safety and success in fishing. Elsewhere too the stone with a hole in it is regarded as of some value.

### I.10.i. Crosses

The cross is a very old sign, much older than Christianity. However, its occurrence in oral tradition in Wessex seems to be largely a result of the Christian influence. This has endowed the cross with a power for good against evil; crossing oneself was and still is held to be a means of protection against evil. The cross also marks the grave, or the site of death. A story from Dorset told of a cross cut in the bark of an oak tree. This marked the spot where a woman had killed herself by throwing herself into a ditch full of water near by. A similar story from Okeford Fitzpaine told of a man who hanged himself in a holly tree. The tree was later marked by a cross. The staff which he carried for protection was propped up against the tree by the man before he hanged himself, being left in such a way that it took root and grew. While the tree and the rooted staff have now been cut down, the informant said that these things had actually been seen. In both stories a suicide's grave has been marked by a cross. This is unusual as the suicide is usually denied any form of Christian burial—the sign of the cross was all they could hope for.

Broadway in Somerset has in the churchyard an old cross with the top broken off. It is said that it was once in the centre of the village, and the steps round it were used by travelling preachers. The broken top is supposed to be buried beneath the crossroads at the centre of the village.

### I.11.i. Curses

Ill luck and even death may result from a curse made verbally or a curse may be intrinsic in the nature of a place or thing. One man cursed himself: this story from Combe St Nicholas should be seen as a kind of moral tale.

G

> There was a story of a man who was riding a big old cart with a big horse. He was wild, and in a very bad temper. He shouted, 'I'll ride to hell.' The horse reared, upset the cart, and the man fell off and broke his neck.

Traditional morality would consign him to hell. If a series of misfortunes occurs at some place, then a previous curse on it may provide a longed-for explanation. Sometimes some actual curse was administered, traditionally by a witch or gipsy. I can remember a gipsy in Cornwall using the threat of a curse to persuade a shopkeeper to buy some of her goods.[2] While the threat in this case was disregarded, there is no doubt that people took the threat of a curse very seriously. A gipsy was said to have thrown a curse on a meadow in the middle of White-church village, Dorset; the curse states that every year when the meadow is being harvested it will rain. The people recalling this tale added that while this has in fact been the case in the majority of years, there have been times when the harvest has been brought in dry. In some oral versions of this story the curse was made by a witch. Literary versions of the story share the theme demonstrated in the story of the man who rode to hell: Dacombe tells us that the curse resulted from the blasphemy of a farmer, who was so cross with his hay for being damp that he swore at it; the point is being made that the field does seem in practice to yield wet hay rather more often than others in the neighbourhood.[3]

One interesting house that has a curse on it is Bettiscombe Manor in the Marshwood Vale, below Pilsdon. The curse does not involve words, but a skull has been at the manor as long as anyone can remember, and its removal is said to cause all sorts of trouble. The tradition is by no means unique to the Wessex area. Udal tells of similar skulls at Chilton Cantelo House, Somerset, and Burton Agnes Hall, Yorkshire.[4] A tradition from Pythouse, Semley, Wiltshire, was collected by the author and will be considered later. Bett also mentions the skull that was kept in the niche in the wall at Burton Agnes Hall, telling the story that the hall was built by three sisters in the time of Queen Elizabeth. The youngest sister was attacked by an outlaw and died before the hall was complete, the sisters having agreed to bury her in the hall:

> They buried her without fulfilling the gruesome compact and strange noises and wild disturbances followed, until, after a space of two years, the body was disinterred, and the skull given a place in the hall. Any attempt to remove it brings trouble in the family.[5]

Bett gives skull stories from Wardley Hall in Lancashire, Tunstead Milton in Derbyshire, and Calgarth Hall, on the bank of Windermere.

The story about Bettiscombe Manor was widely known in both Somerset and Dorset. Television is in part responsible for spreading these traditions, and it is interesting that a modern medium is itself influencing oral tradition. This point is clear from the first version of the tradition collected in Somerset:

> There was a skull in this house, and it was said that if it was taken down the whole house would tumble to the ground. The ITV people went there when a new owner took over the place, who was rather sceptical of the superstition. He decided to take the skull down when challenged about the authenticity of the legend, but there was at once a minor earthquake, and he put it back very quickly.

The interest of the tradition lies in the fact that we know so much about it, and that a good deal has been written about it in the past years. Some of the traditions seem to have developed as a result of false academic research:

> A coloured servant of a man was hard done by, and promises were broken. The servant died, but the body could not be buried at the first attempt. Some years later they tried again, but they still could not bury the body. The skull is still on view in the manor, and it is supposed to scream. It has been on television.

The idea that the skull was formerly a negro slave occurs again in the following version, with an additional piece of information that is also worthy of comment:

> Above the mantelpiece in Bettiscombe Manor, near Bridport, is a very old skull of a negro who is once supposed to have

worked in the house under a very cruel master. The master beat him cruelly, and probably killed him. The story goes that Bettiscombe House changed hands, and the new owner did not like the skull, and he took it and threw it in the pond. After he did this there were terrible noises and screams in the house. There was illness, and the animals died. The new tenant could not stand this so he went out and dragged the pond, and got the skull out and replaced it on the mantelshelf. After this the trouble stopped immediately.

Traditions of this sort often contain the idea that the skull is removed by a sceptic, with unnerving results. However, the present owner of the house, Mr Pinney, told me the following story which is certainly true:

> Not long after I came to the house, a carload of very jovial Australians arrived, saying that their father had been a groom at Bettiscombe, and that they had always been brought up on the story that he was the one who had thrown the skull into the pond with the result that all sorts of things started to go wrong. They had been told to visit the place and see the skull if they ever came to England.

Whether the father was really responsible for throwing the skull in the pond or whether he was continuing a popular tradition, we shall never know. However, it does mean that the story is at least as old as the century, and proably a good deal older—and it has been transmitted round the world.

Bettiscombe Manor was owned with Racedown by the Pinneys. It was built about 1694. The story of the negro comes from the writings of the Dorset folklorist, J. S. Udal, who wrote on the tradition at length in *Dorsetshire Folklore*[6] and in *Proceedings of the Dorset Natural History and Archaeological Society*, vol 31 (1910), pp 176–203. In both of these, Udal puts forward the theory that the skull was that of a negro slave, brought back from the island of Nevis, one of the Leeward Islands, by John Fred Pinney, son of Azariah Pinney, who was transported after the Monmouth rebellion. John returned, having prospered, in about 1800. The supposed maltreatment of the slave fits the folk theme that his skull could not rest and thus cursed the house in some way. Much of this obviously went straight into oral tradition, as Mr Pinney told me that when they first came to the house about thirty years ago the old farmer had pointed out a grille at the back of a cupboard by the fireplace at the west end of the house. He had said that that was where they used to keep the 'black man', and he was fed by having food pushed to him through the bars of the grille. Now the 'negro' version is firmly established in oral tradition, and is strengthened by the additional excitement of the colour of the servant, and the maltreatment of the slave. The truth is far less interesting, and has little chance of acceptance in oral tradition. In 1963 a professor of Human and Comparative Anatomy from the Royal College of Surgeons examined the skull, and classed it as a European skull of a female aged twenty-five to thirty years. It has been suggested that it came from one of the old burial mounds on one of the neighbouring hills, and was perhaps included in the building of the house as a piece of house-luck— thus its strong association with the well-being of the place provided it is not removed.

Further, the skull is associated with the west end of the house though it has never been kept on the mantelpiece. At first it was kept on a beam in the attic, by the chimney brickwork. This beam was sawn off to allow easier access to the attic, after which time it was kept next to the chimney under the roof in the attic. Today it rests in a cardboard box, but still not far from the same chimney. The chimney was the one exit that was always well charmed: the hearth was the centre of the home and needed protection. When first described, in 1840, by a woman who saw it, the skull was white and was kept in the roof; today it is a darker colour, somewhat brown. A legend has been recorded that the skull was in fact that of a young girl who died after a long confinement in the house, but the negro story is more popular.[6] The tradition presents a unique mixture of folklore, research and the oral transmutation of material.

A tradition from Semley, in Wiltshire, is similar in many ways, but has had little or nothing written about it. The story here is given exactly as it was collected:

*Molly of Pythouse*

There is at Pythouse (once the home of Col Benet Stanford) a skeleton which is known as 'Molly'.

Molly is the remains of a female who was hanged at Oxford for the murder of her baby girl by scalding, the father of which is rumoured to have been a member of the Benet Stanford family. The crime is supposed to have been committed in what is known as the 'Pink Room' at Pythouse, which Molly is supposed to haunt, as well as walking in the nearby corridors. There is also a curse which states that should Molly be taken away from Pythouse misfortune will fall upon the family.

Three times Molly has been removed.

The first time a wing of the house caught on fire.

The second time the son and heir died.

The third time the daughter died.

### *1.12.iv. Taboos and undesirable places*

One widespread taboo is the citing of the Devil by name. To say 'the Devil' is the best way to bring him to where you are, so he is often referred to by some other name, such as 'his Satanic Majesty' or 'the Evil One'. On the island of Portland it is taboo to mention the word 'rabbit'. There is a story that the rabbits could cause a great deal of damage with their burrows, thus rendering the quarries unsafe, and had been the cause of more than one fatal accident. While this may be partly true, the rabbit may have had some significance in pagan lore that is still partly remembered.

Sometimes a place has a reputation that makes it undesirable. As such this seems to be a mediatory belief, lying between scepticism and total acceptance. An informant may decide that a certain place has no curse on it, but that it does have evil connections. Similarly a place may be held by some to be haunted, but by others to be simply undesirable. It is an important stage in the development of an oral tradition, and shows the different levels at which a tradition may be held by different people. Traditions are too easily stated, without due allowance being made for the fact that there are often as many versions of the belief as there are informants to tell them. One place near

Ilminster, Somerset, called Wake Hill, is reputed to be haunted; traditions of the haunting will be considered in the following chapter. Of the many informants who mentioned the location, however, several did not consider that the place was actually haunted but rather that there was something unnatural about it:

> This place was not haunted, but it was very creepy, and as a young girl she remembered feeling very frightened, and kept close to her mother, because there were many more trees there than there are now.

Chink nearby shares some of the traditions:

> There was a place called Chink, and the gates above it were called Black Gates. As children they were frightened to go down there, though she did not know why.
>
> Chink was always regarded as a creepy place.

By extension these traditions either develop into full ghost stories or are rationally explained and dismissed.

# CHAPTER 9

# MYTHOLOGICAL TRADITIONS:1

Mythological traditions are popular and widespread in oral lore. Included in this section are fairy lore and ghost lore. The former shows signs of dying out, or at least of being drastically reduced. The latter however seems to be as strong as ever. As with many other traditions survival depends on a degree of acceptability: while fairies are now discredited as feasible beings, fewer people are prepared to dismiss ghosts with such lack of ceremony. Aetiological tales are still told to explain the origins of rocks and natural features and to assign them to mythological causes. It is to these that we turn first.

### J.1.iv. Rocks and stones
The mythological traditions collected relating to rocks and stones were extensive. The stones acquiring these traditions are generally sarsen or standing-stones. Traditions are largely split

into aetiological tales and traditions about the exploits of the stones themselves. This will include their movement, and any special powers they are reputed to have. In the survey a number of aetiological tales were collected concerning the Devil's Stone at Staple Fitzpaine, Somerset. These will illustrate the nature of the tradition. Further traditions from other locations may then be noted.

The Staple Fitzpaine area has several of these large stones, whose origin is something of a mystery. In the folk imagination they are associated with evil, and very often their origin is attributed to either a giant or the Devil. The Staple Fitzpaine stone, now unfortunately moved to widen the road, is in every case attributed to the Devil, which is unusual. Miss Tongue mentions the Devil throwing a stone at a church, in competition with a giant, as explanation for a stone in Hurdlestone Woods on the Mendips.[1] The similarity is striking as the Devil is supposed to have thrown the Staple Fitzpaine stone at the church. The story in oral tradition is to be found in the following forms:

> There is a big stone at Staple Fitzpaine, and the story of how it got there is that when they were building the church the Devil came along with a great bag of stones to lob at the builders. When he got there, however, he found that they had finished the church—the tower was up and everything. He dropped the stones in surprise and left. The biggest stone has been left there, and the rest have been taken away for building and suchlike. The Devil was going to stop the building by throwing the stones at the workmen. The stone is unlucky, and if you prick it it will bleed.

Other versions of the story have it that the stone was actually thrown but fell short. This is a usual theme found in such stories.

> The big stone was called the Devil's Stone. The story was simply that the Devil was supposed to have thrown it from Castle Beacon. If you stick a pin in it it is supposed to bleed, because it has something to do with the Devil.

A similar story shows a little more enthusiasm:

The Devil's Stone was aimed at the church by the Devil, who was up on Castle Neroche. He stood on the beacon, and hurled it down, but he missed. Thus it is in its present position just short of the church. It is supposed to bleed if pricked.

Sometimes the tradition makes a derogatory comment about the Devil's strength:

The stone was rolled by the Devil from Castle Neroche. The Devil however got tired and could roll it no further. It is supposed to bleed if pricked.

Most versions of the story contained the idea that for some reason the stone would bleed if pricked, and some said that the stone had the giant's fingermarks in it. The first version quoted belongs with many other stories, often explaining natural features, where the Devil drops stones or earth, either by accident or because they become too heavy or because he is nonplussed. A number of these will be considered later. The other stories contain the positive if destructive notion of a stone hurled at a church to prevent its completion. The story illustrates well the futility of the Devil's actions. However, the Devil does not only oppose churches. Consider this tale collected in Corfe Castle, Dorset:

The Agglestone rock at Studland is reputed to have been thrown by the Devil from the Isle of Wight, at Corfe Castle, but fell short by five miles or so. There are also some small stones at Rempstone, halfway between Studland and Corfe Castle, which are also supposed to have been aimed at the castle.

Bett has the same story, adding that it is also called 'the Devil's Nightcap', as this is what he in fact threw, and that Agglestone means 'Holy Stone'.[2]

The Hell Stone near Portesham is said to have been thrown by the Devil from Portland, when he was playing quoits.

In some parts of Wessex stories have been recorded that attribute certain stones to the activities of giants. Here stories are more usually told of a giant who drops the stones for some reason, rather than throwing them to cause damage. Versions are known of concerning Porlock and Hawkridge,³ while Giant's Grave, Cheselbourne, Dorset, is supposed to be the grave of a giant who was so upset by his defeat in a stone-throwing contest with another giant that he died and was buried at the spot that now has this name. The contest took place on the top of Nordon Hill, and they had to throw across to Henning Hill, which lies above the spot that marks the site of the Giant's Grave. R. Hunt collected several stories that explained the existence of stones in Cornwall. The granite slabs on the side of St Michael's Mount are a result of the games the giants used to play, hurling large lumps of granite. Similar stories are told of Trecrobben Hill, Lescudjack Hill, while the Lanyon cromlech is generally believed in popular lore to be a giant's quoit.⁴

Stones are not always the result of the Devil or of giants' games. Sometimes they are, or were, people. This tradition is very old, and is found widely in Greek mythology, the best known being in Ovid's *Metamorphoses*. The stones at the entrance to the caves at Wookey are supposed to be the Witch of Wookey and her familiars, who were turned to stones by a priest. More famous are the stones of Stanton Drew. The tradition is that a couple determined to hold their wedding celebrations at the spot. They danced late into the night and the piper told them they should stop, as it was Saturday night, and it would soon be Sunday. However, they were having such a good time that they took no heed. The clock struck, and the piper went. But another took his place, the music increased in pace, and the dancers were compelled by the music to dance. Try as they might they could not stop. The music was provided by the Devil himself, and in the morning all that was to be seen was the three circles of stones.

The Rollright Stones near Chipping Norton are supposed to have resulted from the action of a malevolent witch. An ambitious lord believed that if 'Long Compton I can see, King of England I shall be'. But when the lord and his men reached a place where they could look down over Oxfordshire the witch turned them into a ring of stones. In the Valley of Rocks near

Lynton, Devon, there is a pile of rocks known as Ragged Dick, who with his companions was seized by the Devil and turned into slate for dancing on Sunday.

So much for the origin of the stones. Tradition also has something to say about the nature of the stones themselves. While their origins are mythological their properties are supernatural. Many are thought to have treasure hidden beneath them. They are reputed to move at certain times and some can cure illness. There is supposed to be a stone at Wellington, Somerset, that turns round every time the cock crows, and if you are lucky you may see the treasure that lies beneath it. The stone that marks the Giant's Grave at Cheselbourne, mentioned above, also turns round when the cock crows in the village. The Wimblestones on the Mendips are supposed to be seen dancing round the field under the right conditions. A stone at Stoke-sub-Hamdon, Somerset, moves at midnight:

> When Ham Stone hears the Norton chimes at midnight clack
> It rolls down hill to drink at Jack o' Beards and back.[5]

The Minchinhampton Stone, Gloucestershire, runs round the field in which it is situated when the clock strikes twelve, and at the same time the Whittlestone in the same county goes down to the foot of the hill on which it is situated to drink from the Lady well.[6] The stone at Churchstanton however is so firmly embedded in the earth that a farmer, seeking the treasure that was supposed to lie beneath it, had to give up his attempt to move it despite the fact that he used his strongest horses. He declared that the stone must be 'moored to the roots of the hills'. The only thing that will move such a stone, according to Somerset folklore, is a cock that crows. And it must be a white cock; a black cock will cause nothing but trouble.[7]

The curative properties of stones are not so widely accepted in tradition. Layamon in his *Brut* wrote of Stonehenge:

> The stones are great
> And magic power they have
> Men that are sick
> Fare to that stone

> And they wash that stone
> And bathe away their evil.[8]

Stonehenge was said to be the remains of a giants' dance, rather in the same tradition as Stanton Drew,[9] though others have it that Merlin brought the stones over from Ireland by magic. Whatever the case, they were considered as having particular power. The Crick stone at Morve and the Men-an-tol, both in Cornwall, can cure illness. For the former the patient must be passed through the stone without touching it; it is good for back complaints. The latter cures scrofulous children if they are passed through the stone three times, naked, and then drawn along the grass in an easterly direction three times.

### *J.1.v. Topographical features*

This section is really a continuation of the last, the mythological traditions sharing many of the themes already discussed. The beacon from which the Devil is reputed to have thrown his stone at Staple Fitzpaine has its own tradition. As we have seen, a burial mound naturally becomes a centre for tradition, producing tales of buried treasure and hollowness. The beacon here has become such a treasure mound, though in fact it was never hollow, nor did it contain a grave of any sort. Castle Neroche is a system of earthworks, several ditches and mounds, with a single mound at the northern end commonly called the beacon. The most recent excavation, in 1962 (report yet to be published), confirmed that the earthwork was of Norman and medieval times. Most objects that have been found were dated as being from the twelfth century. By analogy no doubt with other mounds in the area from which bones and goods might have been extracted, Castle Beacon becomes far more than a mere mound of earth, and recurs in traditions in a variety of ways. Under this heading it is hollow and mysterious:

> The beacon itself is hollow, and was built by hand, so runs the legend. There are supposed to be places where you can drop a penny down and hear it drop, that is down rabbit holes. If you put a ferret down in after a rabbit it will never come out again.

Another version has it slightly differently:

> They reckoned that Castle Beacon was hollow inside, and there
> was a place up on the top where you could drop a stone down
> inside and you could hear money rattle.

While the Devil or a giant is often held responsible for the
position of a stone, the Devil is also much blamed for larger
topographical features. The three hillocks at Lambert's Castle
on the borders of Devon and Dorset are called the Devil's Three
Jumps, and one informant told me of three stones near Staple
Fitzpaine that were called the Devil's Stepping Stones. Some
crags near Bodmin in Cornwall are called the Devil's Jump.[10]

The tradition that the Devil drops stones or earth as a result
of the weakness of his apron strings is told of Simons Burrow on
the Blackdown Hills above Wellington in Somerset. The story
goes that there were once five mounds, and the Devil brought
them there in his apron, which broke at that point. Some say,
however, that the five mounds were brought there by the Devil
in the five fingers of his glove. The tradition is found in Mathews,
*Tales of the Blackdown Borderland* (1923), pp 31–3, with the additional information that the barrow was said to commemorate a
stand by Simon, Lord of Exmoor, and that it covered his bones.
This tradition is an old one, though the more popular version
attributes the stones to the Devil. The tradition was current
over 150 years ago.

> I one morning rode over to Black Down, on purpose to inspect
> an immense heap of stones on the top of the hill straight before
> the town [Wellington] which I remembered to have seen when
> I was a boy. The distance from Wellington is about two miles.
> These stones cover about an acre of ground and rise to a great
> height. The country people inform me with great gravity that,
> 'the Devil brought them there in one night in his leather apron.'

Of the other five barrows the writer adds 'The country people
inform me that the Devil brought the five heaps there in his
glove.'[11] Miss Tongue tells the story, adding that the Devil was
going to drop the stones on Wellington Church, but that he had
so many in his apron that the strings broke, and the stones

scattered over an acre of ground and formed the Devil's Lapful, while in a flurry he dropped the rest which formed the five small barrows known as the Devil's Glove. She also writes that it is believed that ill fortune will befall anyone who attempts to take the stones away.[12]

Similar traditions explaining the origin of stones are found in the north of England on Kielder Moor, where there is the Devil's Lapful and on Ilkley Moor the Skirtful of Stones and the Little Skirtful of Stones. Tarr Steps, Exmoor, is also known as the Devil's Bridge. The Devil built it for his own delight, and resolved that no one should use it. Sitting down nearby he pronounced destruction on the first thing to cross over. A cat was sent over and promptly torn to pieces, then followed a vicar carrying a cross and the spell was broken. There followed a verbal contest, and the Devil came off second-best, so he retired, leaving the bridge.

*J.2. Supernatural beings*

If stones were reputed to move it is hardly surprising that oral tradition has attributed certain human characteristics to statues. Again we see the response that ordinary people made to their landowners, whose lives seemed so strange to them. In the grounds of Hinton House, Hinton St George, Somerset, is a statue of Diana. Today it is fast falling into decay, though in its time it must have been something of a wonder. Local tradition has it that when the clock strikes twelve, Diana gets down off her column and goes down to drink the waters. The carved dogs at the entrance to Bryanston House, by Blandford Bridge, Dorset, are similarly supposed to climb down from their perches and drink from the River Stour.

*J.2.i. Devils, appearances and associates*

The Devil has already appeared in the many traditions concerned with the origins of stones. In some cases however the story is really about the Devil, and the motif of the stone is only incidental. Three more versions concerning the Devil's Stone at Staple Fitzpaine were collected, these taking the Devil as their main motif rather than the stone he threw. A similar tale is told of Broadway Church, with an addition to explain the position of the church now:

> The Devil was cross with the people of Broadway, and he threw three stones from Castle Neroch. One landed just down Hare Lane, the second at Staple Fitzpaine, and the third, well he could not remember where that one landed. The people of Broadway, however, to be safe, moved the church from the centre of the village to where it is now. Old Nick wasn't a very good shot in any case because all the stones missed their mark.

The Devil may appear in person, often as a warning or as a sign of evil. The stories told of dancers who profaned the sabbath being turned into stones have their echo in this tradition from Ash, Somerset:

> This was a story from the informant's mother. One Saturday night the woman was scrubbing the floor, and by mistake she continued after midnight. As she threw the water out she always swore that she saw the Devil. She came from a very religious family.

At Crimchard, near Chard, there was an old ruined chapel. There it was said the Devil appeared to one of Cromwell's soldiers in the shape of a filthy hog. Standing stones are sometimes, of course, also associated with the appearance of the Devil; the stone at Churchstanton had this reputation. Many years ago a party of people had been on a visit to Bakers Farm, and had left just before midnight. Some of the girls ran on in front. One of them jumped on the stone and said, 'Now, Mr Devil, it's about twelve o'clock, and it's time if you were likely to come.' In a second she regretted what she had said for an animal like a huge calf began to bellow, and they all ran away. It pursued them home and they did not dare venture out until daylight.[13]

Miss Tongue told me a story that was very similar, though placed versions of it at both Staple Fitzpaine and at Combe St Nicholas. It has been established earlier in this book that there is no Devil's Stone at Combe St Nicholas and while there

is no reason to disbelieve that the story could be true of Staple
Fitzpaine, the similarity with the tale recorded from Churchstanton leads one to presume that there was a degree of confusion in the mind of the informant. The version Miss Tongue
provided was nevertheless a good tale:

> Someone had summoned the Devil rather in the same manner
> as they did at Staple. However, the Devil chased them and they
> ran away in terror. One wanted to stop at the cross-roads, as
> they thought that it would be safer. However, the others said
> that it was not a safe cross-roads, and made him run on. They
> ran on a little and waited. They heard a yell and then there
> was silence. The Devil had come for the suicide who was buried
> at the cross-roads, and who had foolishly been placed there
> without a stake through his heart.

It is not always the Devil who has the advantage. Susceptible
to cold, he is said to have died from the freezing conditions on
top of Windwhistle in winter, and that is why it is called
by that name. Some say that he is buried beneath the hills. In
Northumberland at Birtley there is the Devil's Stone, with the
marks of the Devil upon it. From this stone the Devil leapt
across the Tyne, but he misjudged the distance and fell into the
river at a place called Leap Crag Pool. However, not many
traditions hold that the Devil is dead. One Somerset informant
had this to say:

> 'Stories about the Devil? No, I can't say as I've heard much
> on that.'
>   'But have you heard where he is supposed to be?'
>   'Oh yes, I can tell 'e that. He's here in the village for the
> most part.'

### J.2.iii. Witches

Witches are not easy to classify, and the procedure adopted was
to take the division between black, grey and white, with a
general group for traditions that do not distinguish the type of
witch discussed. The black witch was the one that did evil,
frightening the local inhabitants, who placated her with free

H

milk and other food. Her (or his) practices included the casting the evil eye, by which power they could inflict illness or even death on people. More usually the illness of cattle and failure of crops could be ensured by a timely spell. Grey witches were in a sense worse than black ones, because one never knew where one was with them: they could be beneficent or maleficent as they chose. A white witch was one who put her powers to good use, to cure ailments, to bless cattle and to give good crops.

The witches of oral tradition are very different from historical witches of a few centuries ago. In fact it is sometimes difficult to say whether some of them were ever real witches at all. Any slightly eccentric old lady, living by herself, who dabbled in herbs and could charm warts, could easily win the reputation of being a witch. If she chose to exploit the situation, she could build up a reputation and perhaps gain a living that depended largely on being held in awe by the local inhabitants. Alternatively, any old lady who did not go to church and seemed unpleasant could be blamed for any number of ills, supposedly the product of her spells, and this might result in action being taken against her. Similarly, while the historical witch can be either male or female, it is a fact that the witch of oral tradition seems to be more often than not a woman. Practising witches are certainly not extinct; I have met a grey witch myself in Wiltshire. However, the witchcraft of oral tradition rests on suspicion and popular belief rather than the 'real thing', and as such should be seen as a popular version of, rather than the heart of, the occult.

Many places yielded traditions of a general nature about witches. Miss Tongue gave me this version of the Pitminster witch:

> This witch at Pitminster was met by the informant when she was a child. The witch used to have toad familiars, and she was really a mental case. However, Miss Tongue used to like her toads and cuddled them in the middle of the road. The witch could have no ill effect on her because she was a 'chime child'.

Also collected by personal interview was a tradition that showed the very real effect that witchcraft had on the ordinary people:

> The informant had heard from her father that Combe St Nicholas was a very superstitious place, and they certainly believed in witches there. One day her father's mother had come home, and she was very cross. She said, 'What have you been doing? I met so and so up in the village, and she said that you had bewitched her, that she came downstairs at twelve o'clock at night, and there was a hook in the way, and that you were there, and that you had bewitched her.' And she was terrified of him.

The tale as it was given lacks some coherence, and it is not clear who was supposed to have done the bewitching. The last story shows how easily a witch story could become established in the folk tradition:

> There used to be an old girl who lived up the lane who was called Welsh. Some of the locals were afraid to go past her house. The informant said that he had once courted a girl who lived in the area, and she was afraid to walk past the house.

### J.2.iii.a. Witches, black

Tales of the evils perpetrated by black witches are popular in tradition, partly because they often include some fairly dramatic escape on the part of the witch. There follows a typical example, from Stathe, Somerset. The inn mentioned is still to be seen.

> There was an old woman who had a reputation for being a witch. She cast spells on the farmer's crops and animals, and the locals got so fed up with this state of affairs that they went out to set on her. She saw them coming, however, and to avoid arrest she disappeared up the chimney, burning her smock on the way up. She then disappeared over the moors as a hare. The local inn remembers the story with the name, 'The Black Smock'.

Witches were supposed to be able to 'shape change', that is to form themselves into the shape of an animal. The animal that was their constant companion was known as the 'familiar', though it is not unknown for the witch to change shape into the familiar. The familiar is traditionally a hare, a rabbit or sometimes a fox. A cat is less common. Toads were also found, and there is perhaps a hint of this in the story quoted above from Miss Tongue. It is thus considered unlucky to kill any animal that may be associated with a witch, in case it is in fact a witch having changed its shape. A witch story from Bridgwater told of a woman who turned herself into a white rabbit. The men of the locality determined to catch her, and did, in fact, corner the rabbit. One man went to catch the animal and gave it a debilitating kick, but the rabbit escaped. Next day the old woman was confined to her bed, nursing a bad leg, the result of the kick she had received in the shape of the rabbit. Another story from Exmoor told of a woman who changed her shape to that of a fox, so she could rob a farmer's hen-run. The farmer lay in wait for her one night and shot her, using silver bullets as they were the only ones that would be effective. But the witch managed to escape, though badly wounded. No one was quite sure who the witch was, but a few days later the postman explained that the woman who lived in the cottage some miles away, and who was known to be something of a recluse, had been taken to Minehead hospital, and some said that her leg was found to be full of silver shot. She later pined away and died. If a witch loses blood, she loses her power, and will shortly die.[14]

A story from Spettisbury, Dorset, shows the effect that a reputation for being a witch could have on the community, emphasising the fact that many women who acquired this reputation were in fact evil people who scrounged a living off their neighbours by making them fear their supposed powers:

> There was a woman who lived in the village, and all the farmers believed that she was a witch. To keep in her favour they supplied her with eggs and cheese, and other farm produce. Her powers were that she could stop animals like sheep and cows from passing her doorway. She was able to stop them dead with

a fixed stare. She would sit in her front room all day long and watch people go by.

### *J.2.iii.b. Witches, grey*

Two other stories collected had the theme of the witch being able to transfix animals and thus prevent them from passing her door. These witches are classified as grey as the informant in each case did not emphasise their evil nature as strongly as was done in the traditions considered above. Both stories come from south Somerset:

> There was a witch that lived in a cottage. One day she put a curse on a farmer's pigs, as he'd got on the wrong side of her. The pigs refused to go past the cottage when he drove them down the road.

The other story is more simple still:

> There was, the informant had heard, a witch who lived at Knowle St Giles, and horses were troublesome and were afraid to go past her door.

In one story of this sort heard in conversation, a witch used to transfix the baker's cart and while it was stopped, nip out and steal a loaf, and then allow it to carry on again.

### *J.2.iii.c. Witches, white*

White witches are often simply people who can perform various cures, predict events, especially the weather, or have the ability to bless crops and cattle. Though they do not use their powers for evil purposes, they are remembered in oral tradition, and sometimes stories of their abilities get handed down to future generations. Consider this story, collected from near Broadway, Somerset:

> There was a witch who lived up on Ham Hill, on the left down a small lane, now overgrown, in a cottage that is now a ruin. People of society used to come from miles around to have their fortunes told.

Another witch told of in tradition at Ashill nearby attributed to the witch the power of blessing the cattle:

A woman used to come up to the farm from time to time, and the farmer gave strict instructions that no one was to speak to her or to stop her. She looked at the cows and smiled at a labourer. In other words she was blessing the cattle, and she was a white witch.

The white witch had her place in the community, and in her own way was important. In many respects the rise of the Welfare State and modern methods of nursing threatened her position:

There was a story about an old midwife that the informant had heard from her mother. This woman was supposed to be a witch, and people always called her to a birth for fear of offending her, and thus bringing harm to the child. Thus, though unqualified, she officiated as midwife in the area for years. This was called 'overlooking the baby'. A compromise was reached when a qualified doctor was present at the event, and the old woman would come and look after the mother and child for the ten days that followed. Old knives and scissors were put on the staircase at the time of the full moon, when she was supposed to be walking. But she was never known to do any harm. One day a man saw a hare, and the witch was always supposed to be able to turn into a hare, so he threw a stone at it, hit it, but only knocked it. The next day the woman had a bruise on her forehead.

This story, that comes fron Hinton St George, Somerset, is an interesting mixture of probable details and folk tradition. The old knives and scissors were traditional items placed on the stairs or more usually under the doormat to keep evil spirits away—yet the informant insists that the woman had never been known to do harm. The addition of the shape-changing motif is an interesting piece that shows the beginnings of the development of an oral tradition in its own right.

### *J.2.iv. Giants*

Several giants have so far been mentioned in connection with topics in other classifications. But the Cerne Abbas giant has not yet been included, and he is an important subject in Wessex tales. Cerne Abbas, Dorset, has a huge 180ft giant cut in the turf of a steep hillside near the town. The exposed stones and earth are chalky, so the white figure stands out as a local landmark. The story of its origin is that a great giant caused much trouble throughout the area, and the local inhabitants of Cerne Abbas either slew him on the spot where the figure is to be seen today, and then traced his outline in the turf, or drew his likeness there as a memorial to his great size. The figure certainly lacks proportion, and its unmistakable phallic emphasis leads many to the conclusion that it was some sort of fertility god. While its exact age is unknown, it is certainly very old, and it has been subject to 'scourings', a custom accompanied by some merriment during which the outline of the giant was cleared of weeds and grass. The sexual aspect of the giant is emphasised by the local tradition that barrenness in women may be cured if the woman sits on the right part of the giant's figure, though some say that it is necessary to have sexual intercourse on the carving of the giant to ensure success. Modern tradition still warns young girls not to picnic in the area. A nineteenth-century vicar stopped the scourings, as the festivities accompanying them tended to demonstrate too much the traditional view that the giant was a fertility god.

The maypole for Cerne was traditionally placed in the Trendle, a squarish earthwork on the hill above the giant; it was perhaps once associated with its fertility cult of the giant, and was certainly connected with it in more recent times through the maypole observances. Modern authorities tend to date the giant as of the Romano-British period, being a version of the Roman god Hercules, who in turn was derived from the Greek god Heracles. The god often has a club in one hand and a lion skin in the other. The Cerne giant has a club in one hand, and his other hand is outstretched as if he once held something. While the origins of the giant are still uncertain, the traditions about him are retained.

### J.3. Fairies

There remains little oral tradition relating to fairies in Wessex, though stories are remembered from literary sources, the latter being an indication of the ubiquitous nature of such beliefs up to the earlier part of this century. Dorset however provided one fine fairy story, apparently still in oral tradition:

> There is a superstition that surrounds the small door and tiny staircase in the church [Stourpaine, Blandford Forum]. It is believed that the fairies or elves make the bells ring in the church. The entrance to the bell tower was supposed to have been made so as to allow the fairies or elves to go up to the bells and make them ring. They are supposed to do this early in the morning by using the fresh dew off the grass. It is said that if the fairies see the footprints of a mortal in the grass on entering the stairs to the bell tower, then that person has extremely bad luck, and further the bells will not ring. Generally no one will enter this small passage, but if they do so they only do it when the dew is off the grass. There is also a superstition that if one is very quick, as soon as the dew is off the grass, and enters the small door, one might see tiny drops of dew that the fairies or elves dropped as they hurried up the stairs.

There is little difference made in current oral tradition between pixies and fairies, though elves are more unusual. Wessex fairies on the whole are an unpleasant lot and as such are at least dying out largely uncorrupted by romanticism.

### J.10. Spirits

Will o' the Wisp or Jack the Lantern stories are still common in Wessex, though few people actually believe that the light is a spirit. This subject has already been considered in Chapter 7 (H.2), but oral tradition lacks any of the more complicated tales where a person is misled by the light, usually ending up in a wet cold bog. Such a tale is found in *Forgotten Folk Tales of the English Counties*, by Miss Tongue (pp 81ff and 159ff), though oral tradition had shorter tales to offer at the time of this survey:

> The informant had heard people say that they had seen this light affair, and that as fast as you went, the faster this light

would go also. He thought that it was probably their imagination, but people did think that they had seen it, and it would disappear over the hedge, and they would not be able to find where it had gone. He had heard several people talk about this. They used to call it 'Jack the Lantern'. Mrs B. had heard of 'fairy talk' about Jack the Lantern, but not at Dowlish Wake, and she did not know what it was, or anything about it.

Will o' the Wisps are held to be not only the souls of unbaptised infants, but also the spirits of the dead in general. Stoke Pero Church, Exmoor, is a place where the Spunkies are supposed to come, showing a watcher there on Hallowe'en who this year's ghosts will be.

*J.10.ii. House spirit, hob*
A hob is a general term for a house spirit of a friendly nature. In line however with the etymology of the word, this section has been used to classify spirits, or more generally ghosts, associated specifically with particular houses. 'Hob' was formerly a name for a rustic or clown, and thus 'Robin Goodfellow or Puck, a hobgoblin, a sprite or elf'. Hobgoblin becomes 'a terrifying apparition, a bogy'.[15] In more than one case it will be seen that the hob is most likely a poltergeist, and is even described as such. Tradition tends to place such phenomena firmly with such things as ghosts, and it therefore seems best to include the poltergeist in this section.

The typical tradition of the hob or house spirit is told of a large and often old house. Most big old houses were found in the survey to have a ghost of some sort. Often a simple hob type of ghost was found, though where tradition had had a chance to develop the informant told of a named ghost, such as in the form of a Grey Lady (see J.12). Hinton House, Hinton St George, was an example of the general type of tradition.

There was a room in the house that was haunted, and it was called the 'haunted room'.

There was a ghost in the house, and his Lordship himself had told them all once that he himself had seen the ghost.

Room 23 in the house was always the haunted room. It was called the 'ghost room'. The informant had no idea who the ghost was, or any other details about it.

Half a dozen tales of this general sort were collected in the area. Similar general traditions were collected about Clayhanger House, Combe St Nicholas, 'the big house' Cury Mallet, the Manor House, Dowlish Wake, the Grove at Stocklinch; these serve only as examples , for there were many others in the area of the survey. Sometimes the traditions told contained greater detail, offering more narrative appeal. The Holman Clavel Inn on the Blackdowns, for example, has a friendly hob who is called 'Charlie':

> Up at the Holman Clavel pub years ago, this place was sort of haunted, and this went on for years. It was nothing for them to hear the skittles in the alley, but when they went in they would find nothing. At first the younger ones thought that it was someone playing about. But as it went on, and no one was seen, the older people said that it was 'Old Charlie'. He was perhaps an old man who had died and had stayed there. Further they would sometimes wash up the glasses at night, but leave them on the counter to dry, to be packed away in the morning. Next morning they would find every cup put back in place. The landlady began to find this rather annoying, and could not stand it any longer. She thought that Charlie must be turning up after wash day, as she had her clothes in from the line, and folded up ready to iron. When she came in next morning everything was ironed and folded up for her. Though they tried to find someone playing a trick, they never did, and the old people used to say, 'It's Old Charlie.'

A literary version tells of a spirit in a Blackdown inn, but the writer does not say if it is the same one. In this story a voice summoned a young lady. She fearfully took a Bible, and having read a verse to protect herself asked the voice what it wanted. The spirit indicated where a quantity of wealth was hidden, and the girl was rewarded for her former kindness by being shown the money.[16] Whether this is another version of the Old Charlie story is not clear, but the landlord of the Holman Clavel told me that Old Charlie still turns up sometimes, usually when some strangers on holiday from London or elsewhere are sceptical about him: then Old Charlie moves about a little.

The notion that a house spirit is some sort of a poltergeist is often indicated by the nature of the tradition. Sometimes this is merely hinted at:

> There was supposed to be a haunted house between Hinton and Crewkerne. The people who lived there before the ones who do now used to have their weaving press moved.

In other cases, however, the reported events that led to the establishment of the story are marked by the usual traits of a poltergeist presence. Chink, just outside Ilminster, is a good example of this. There was originally a house here that is now pulled down:

> There was a ghost associated with the ruined house at the bottom of Chink, where things used to get thrown about. As a child the informant could remember playing in the ruins of the house that had been abandoned. He was not afraid, but of course they did not go there at night.

> They said that no one was able to live in the old house, and that there was a poltergeist there. It used to torment the place, and clothes put down at night would not be there next day. The last people gave up in desperation, and the place was turned into a cattle stall.

While there is now no trace of the buildings, the place still has a very bad reputation, and is associated with a suicide and a more general haunting that will be considered later. Wood Court, on the other hand, is an interesting example of a building still standing, that had locally a bad reputation for being haunted. It gives this tradition about its house spirit:

> Wood Court has a reputation for being haunted, or more exactly for having a poltergeist, as the spirit is never seen. Footsteps have been heard going up the stairs, and doors have been heard opening and shutting. One day there was a terrific noise outside the back door, but no one was to be found. The poker jumps in the grate, and one night the light started to swing

round and round for no reason. They were playing cards late into the night and the visitors, strangers in the services, were scared out of their wits, and lost their concentration, and did badly at cards. The front and back doors were kept open wide by the previous owner to allow the spirit easy access in and out of the house. By the house was a ruined chapel, once used for making cider, and it was thought that the desecration of this place might have had something to do with the presence of the poltergeist.

Still current in the oral tradition in parts of Dorset near Durweston is an event that at one time caused some local interest. It is a good example of the processes by which an occurrence which to some extent is documented passes into tradition, and becomes both transmitted and transmuted. The traditions generally run something like this:

> One of the two houses on Norton Hill had a 'force'. The table was said to clear itself if it was set for meals, and a vase was seen to return to the window sill when removed from the table. In some stories boots are reported to have flown to their cupboard when taken out. It was said that boots and shoes were thrown out of the house as fast as the owners could throw them back again. Some say that these happenings were the result of two orphan girls staying in the house; they lived and died there. They were living with the owner, an honourable gentleman who was believed locally for his explanation.

Traditions varied in the details of the events, though many were more insistent that the strange happenings were a result of the two girls:

> A pair of orphan girls were adopted and came to live at a lonely house at Norton, known as 'The Folly'. The girls aroused a poltergeist. Amongst other strange happenings there was on several occasions the sound of very heavy footsteps that seemed to approach the house and then go away again. But no person was seen. On these occasions a slate would be found in the garden with the words, 'Mon in Gar'. This was thought to mean that there was money hidden in the garden, but after a thorough search nothing was found.

Several versions were collected. In one the slate was only found once, and the inscription was 'Money in Garden'. It was also reported that the children moved to Iwerne Minster when the old man died, and that when they finally moved back to London the poltergeist subsided. The most accurate informant actually dated the event correctly, while another updated it as the following story shows:

> During World War II two girls were evacuated from London, and were brought to live at Norton with an elderly married couple. On their arrival a poltergeist was aroused, and during its activities a piece of slate was found implying that there was money buried in the garden of the house in which they were staying. In spite of repeated attempts to find the money, nothing was found. The poltergeist was still active when the old man of the house died. The two children then went to live elsewhere at Durweston, and the poltergeist followed them there. After the war the two children went back to London, and the poltergeist was 'laid'.

This process of updating is found elsewhere, and it will be noticed that the theme of hidden treasure is becoming almost as important as the poltergeist itself. The event occurred in the winter of 1894–5, and it has been well documented by various writers; a full account is given in the *Western Gazette*, 11 January 1895. The children were fostered out to a widow, Mrs Best. The disturbances were investigated by the Society for Psychical Research, which mentioned the flying boots. The rector of Durweston and the schoolmaster visited the house one night and reported strange vibrations and knockings. It was at this time that the poltergeist, on being asked to communicate with them, produced the slate with the words 'money' and 'garden' on it, scratched in chalk. The elder child was moved to Iwerne Minster where the noises followed her. Eventually the poltergeist became so disturbing that an inspector responsible for foster-children was sent for and the child was taken back to London, where she was examined by a doctor who found her consumptive and hysterical. Traditions show remarkable detail that is not so far removed from reported fact at the time. The whole story is a strange one that will no doubt linger in folk memory. What happened to the girls is not known, but there was no doubt a great deal of suffering in the incident that the lapse of time has not altogether erased.[17]

*J.10.vi. Animal spirits*
One of the most common traditions about animal spirits has a black dog as its central motif. Very often the black dog is a warning or a death omen. There are many black-dog stories in Wessex—though they are by no means the only animal spirits found in oral lore. Black dogs are sometimes simply mentioned in tradition as being at a certain location, and as bringing bad luck. A black dog is reported at Castle Neroche, and another below Dommett, on the Blackdowns. Another was supposed to be seen at Hinton St George, and one informant told of one at Westport. There are black dogs reported from Bishop's Lydeard (1968), at the witch tree, Stogursey, Weacombe in the Quantocks, Winsford Hill (Exmoor), and on the sea road from St Audries to Perry Farm. This was sighted in 1960. A large, strange, light-coloured dog was seen in the vicinity of Porlock in 1910 on a couple of occasions, and each time there was a death in the neighbourhood.[18] On the Devon–Dorset border at Uplyme a tradition was found about a black dog that had been part of the family circle in a house. Although the dog did no harm, the farmer was eventually taunted by his friends to get rid of the ghostly animal. He chased the dog and where the animal vanished a quantity of money was found. The dog is remembered in the name of an inn still to be seen at the side of the road. Udal in *Dorsetshire Folklore* (pp 167ff) gives the story in more detail and states that it was last seen according to his source in 1856.

Not all black dogs are taken as warnings. Some seem to be more simply the ghosts of dead animals. A series of stories was collected from Blandford Forum concerning a dog that ran up the road to Salisbury towards Pimperne.

> There is a ghost dog that runs recklessly from the base of Letton Hill to Pimperne with much chain rattling. It is invisible but

thought to be a dog, as people who have reached out in an effort to halt the ghost have felt nothing but soft fur.

The dog is interesting because it is usually invisible, but may be heard, and the tradition usually includes a reference to the touching of the fur. The same story was also told five miles away at Tarrant Gunville, though in this case the chain was grabbed, and instead of feeling hard like iron was as soft as velvet. Blandford Bridge is reputed to be haunted by a black dog of the more common sort, while Stourpaine offers another ghost dog, with a traditional explanation:

> There is supposed to be a dog that runs from the village square to the Latch. The dog had apparently been well treated in its early life, but when its owner moved across the hill it was given to another. The other owner who lived around the square treated the dog badly and tied it with a chain. The dog tried many times to escape from its imprisonment, and one day it did . It ran through the square with its chain dragging behind it. Just as it rounded the corner a horse-drawn waggon came round the corner, trampling the dog before it had time to get away. The dog died, and there is supposed to be the ghost of this dog. It cannot be seen, but all that can be heard is the rattling of the chain, as it runs to its old master. Strangely enough the dog does not disappear when it reaches the place where it died, but it runs on to the Latch, up on the side of Hod Hill. There it is believed that the dog spent many happy times with its old master.

This tradition has some similarity with the Pimperne ghost dog, in that the dog could not be seen. Such animals are sometimes guardians, dating perhaps from the time when a dog was sacrificed beneath a road or bridge to ensure safe passage. They are certainly very different from the black dogs that tradition assigns quite firmly with the Other World creatures; these are given a grim character in oral tradition, and are usually associated with death. Some stories found simply tell of the phantom dog as a visitor from the Other World who warns or tells of death:

> There is a lane above Chaffcombe [Somerset] that leads to the Happy Inn. There was a person called Hallet, who lived at

Lidmarsh, and his wife was coming through this way one night during the First World War. She saw a black dog with a chain, and the next day she received notification that her son had been killed. There were no other stories about a black dog being seen at this place.

Near Selworthy a black dog is supposed to have resulted from the action of the sexton when carrying a coffin to Selworthy Church from Horner Mill. One of the handles of the coffin worked loose, and he banged it in again with a stone. The screws must have penetrated the corpse's head and allowed the ghost to escape, and this now appears in the form of a black dog.[19]

Many other traditions were collected that told of super-natural animals, and in oral tradition today in Wessex these seem to be as popular as the better-known black dog. Often the animal's characteristics were apparent:

An animal, a cross between a donkey and a dog, was supposed to be seen at times near Buckland St Mary [Blackdowns]. A fatal accident befalls the person who sees this, but he always lives to tell the tale that he has seen the animal. For those who lived in the Grange at Buckland, if they saw a white dog then they knew a fatality would befall them. The informant's own mother had seen this grey [*sic*] dog and had gone to put her hand on him, and he had disappeared. Then something would happen to the owners of the Grange.

This tradition is a mixture of two stories, that have become somewhat confused in the telling. Another tradition from several miles away shows certain similarities:

The informant's grandmother had told her about a donkey in Cricket Lane [Cricket Malherbie, Somerset]. They used to walk in those days, and the informant's grandmother lived up at the Grange at Buckland. The grandmother had a step-mother who had her child at the same time as she, the grand-mother, had her first child. The stepmother died, leaving the child. The informant's grandmother put her own baby in a cart, and was walking to Buckland to fetch her newly born step-brother, who was by then nearly six weeks old, with the intention of bringing him back to look after him. In the early light of the morning she started off. She reckoned that this donkey walked down the road beside her. The donkey was supposed to be the dead mother's ghost.

Supernatural horses also appear, and many of these will be considered with their riders in human forms later. At Otterford, however, there is supposed to be a white horse breathing fire, and also a dog; they go through a certain gate without opening it. But not all animal spirits are so frightening. This tale comes from Curland, several miles south-east of Taunton.

> One night a farmer was coming home late on horseback. Suddenly a young foal appeared which was not recognisable as belonging to anyone in the area. The farmer had great trouble in keeping the foal away from his own horse. At last they reached home, and the farmer allowed the foal to follow his own horse into the field. He unsaddled and took the bridle off, and took them inside. He told his wife about the foal, and returned with the lantern in order to see better. However, the foal had completely disappeared, and next morning there were no footprints, nor any trace of the foal to be found, and no one in the area knew of anyone who had lost such a foal. It was supposed to have been bay in colour and to have had a white face.

Another story from Corfe near Taunton told of another night encounter:

> One night, coming home very late, the informant was followed by a very large dog. It kept behind him at about five yards. It was brown and apparently normal. It followed him to his house, where on opening the door and letting the light out, the dog completely disappeared. Other strange things have been reported on this road.

In both cases the animal spirit disappears when light is introduced, though both of these tales may be based on actual incidents that have since become marked with traces of primitive belief in the telling.

From Donhead St Andrew, Wiltshire, comes a more dramatic story:

I

When first married I lived in a cottage up Fetch Common way. The bedroom had wall cupboards in opposite corners of the room, and something used to pass from one cupboard across to the other. The 'thing' was large, dark and animal-like.

Blandford Forum has the ghost of a sheep perhaps without a head, that runs up and down Sheep Market Hill, by the church, at midnight. Some versions had it that it was to be seen by the old grammar school, near an old burial ground. The sheep market was moved out of the town in 1822, and while the story is to be found in literary sources, it is still found in oral tradition with the typical variations; so as a tale it must date from at least that time.

Ghost horses of a less terrifying sort than the one reported from Devon have been heard at Ashley Wood, on the road between Blandford and Wimborne, and in Somerset on Windwhistle. In the first story a man was in the woods with his dog, and suddenly the dog growled, bared his teeth, and put his tail between his legs:

Then was heard the sound, not unlike that of galloping horses. They went on, and next morning the man went back to the spot, but saw no hoof marks or any signs of horses.

Legg tells a very similar story about Down Wood, a few miles nearer Blandford.[20] The similarity in detail is striking, but it is not possible that my informant read it there, as Mr Legg's book was published after the survey was concluded in Dorset.

# MYTHOLOGICAL TRADITIONS:2

## J.11. Ghosts

We come now to one of the largest bodies of belief extant in oral lore. The ghost story is ubiquitous. To relate all the traditions collected that included ghost lore would be a considerable task, but it is necessary to consider something of their nature.

Under the general heading of J.11 come the very brief traditions that are often no more than a comment. Belief in the ghost is not necessarily indicated, and frequently an informant was at pains to point out that 'it was only said that . . .' or, 'some people said that . . .'. Alternatively, they would end with a comment like 'but that's just a tale we were brought up on, mind'. Nevertheless, the ghost story, and particularly the one that is simple and involves little more than a direct haunting, keeps a strong place in oral tradition which modern life does not seem able to erode with the same effectiveness as it does the fairy story. Further, some ghost stories seem to be the result of comparatively recent events like road accidents, and these seem to replace older stories that have perhaps become lost or forgotten. The general traditions included under this classification have of course little narrative worth: the ghosts are without name, without sex, and without any special characteristic. They have no story to explain their existence, and as such take the lowliest place in the hierarchy of the ghost story. There follow a few examples to illustrate the point:

Barrington Priory, Somerset.
The informant had heard that there was some sort of a ghost at the Priory, but no details were known.

Chard, Somerset.
There was supposed to be a ghost of some sort in a doctor's surgery at Chard. The informant did not know which room was haunted. However, it was said that one room was not used because it was thought to be haunted.

Hanford House, Dorset.
A twelve o'clock on New Year's Night the informant had been told that you would hear the chains rattle, and then the ghost of the house walked.

Winterborne Kingston, Dorset.
Somewhere in the older part of the village there is a haunted gate where two people were run down by a terrified horse.

Altogether thirty-six of these simple tales were collected in the area of the detailed survey, and no doubt other areas of similar size would yield equal quantities. For all their simplicity, the stories are told and handed down from one generation to another. There is no attempt to entertain the hearers, or even to astonish them. Such stories seem to get told because the teller knows something that he feels the hearer might not know, and that to pass on knowledge, however doubtful it may seem, is a means whereby the teller can establish himself. We all love to pass on something, even if we first apologise for its existence.

*J.11.i. Meetings with ghosts*

Where traditions concerning ghosts contain some detail of the circumstances and conditions of the encounter, the result is often a more interesting narrative. Two traditions collected told of meetings with ghosts that were many hundreds of years old. The first is told of the Quantock Hills above Cothelstone:

> On the road down to Cothelstone from the crest which runs along the Quantocks there, there is a tradition of a mounted warrior on a white horse, with clanking armour. Quite a number of people used to go up to the pub there for folk singing. They argued about the ghost. Some said that it was a lad having fun with a horse and chains. But one old man had told the informant how once when he was young he had been up to the pub one evening, and the time had come to walk back to Milverton. It was quite late at night. He was walking along the top—it was much wilder then—when he heard someone shouting and the thunder of some horse's hooves. He looked round to see who the mad man was, thinking that it was someone who was tight. There he saw, chasing down towards him, a man on a horse, and the man had plaits. He ran from the top at Park End to the bottom towards Bishops Lydeard.
>
> Someone else had said that they had heard shouting and the noise of a galloping horse on this stretch of road, and it was a place where one was careful.

This is an interesting story and would appear to be a retention in the folk memory of an event that took place over 1,000 years ago. By all accounts it would seem that the rider referred to is a Danish invader. It is almost certain that the Danes landed in this part of Somerset, though just where exactly they went has not been established. The *Anglo-Saxon Chronicle* reports that the Danes were active in the Bristol Channel area in the year AD 894, and there was a battle at Watchet in AD 918 when a large party of them was driven off with much slaughter. They returned in 987 and laid waste the town. They plundered Somerton as early as 877. Traditions that red hair is unlucky by association with the Danes have been discussed already (see Chapter 5). The Danes did not fight on horseback, as we know

from poems like the *Battle of Maldon*, though they may have
carried out raids on horseback. The dress of the warrior is too
vague to be of much help, and while the Danes wore armour,
the plait sounds more of a traditional than a historical coiffure.
There is however a story in tradition that mentions the Danes
at Dowsborough Camp, which is not far from Cothelstone.[1] It
is possible that a memory survives here of a Danish invader.

The tale is worth comparing with the following story from
near Cranborne, Dorset; it is included in a publication of the
Dorset Natural History & Archaeological Society called *Dorset
Barrows*, where the author tells a story given to him by Dr
R. C. C. Clay, and dating from the winter of 1927–8. Briefly the
encounter took place at night while he was driving along the
road from Cranborne to Handley, about 150yd past Squirrel's
Corner. He saw a horseman to the north-east, travelling in the
same direction as himself, and when finally the horseman came
within fifty yards of the road he saw that it was no ordinary
horseman:

> . . . for he had long bare legs, and wore a long loose coat. The
> horse had a long mane and tail, but I could see no bridle and
> stirrups. The rider's face was turned toward me but I could not
> see his features. He seemed to be threatening me with an imple-
> ment which he waved in his right hand above his head.

The rider disappeared soon after and, noting the spot, it was
found next day to be the site of a low round barrow. Other
reports are mentioned of persons being troubled by a threatening horseman in the area.[2] The implication is that this is the
ghost of a prehistoric man, which makes him a very old ghost
indeed. What is mainly lacking in this tradition and in the
Cothelstone story is further authentically collected versions of
the encounter to establish the position of the tales in extant
oral tradition.

By contrast with these old stories, here is a very recent tale
from Sturminster Newton; the event from which the story
developed took place in August 1965. Apart from being an
example of modern folk tale, showing that ghost stories retain

their popularity, it is an example of the growing lore resultant from the death toll exacted by the motor car.

> Three years ago there was an accident on Sturminster Bridge. A mini crashed with a heavy lorry, and the occupants of the mini were killed; three people. One night about a year ago a boy was riding a motor cycle along the road past the bridge when three figures stepped out in front of him. They appeared too suddenly for him to stop, and he ran right into them. However, he just passed straight through them, and when he looked behind him they had disappeared.[3]

### 7.11.iii. Ghosts as men

The given sex of a ghost indicates that a good deal more is known about the haunting than its supposed existence. Stories that talk of the ghost of a man usually have some explanation to offer for its existence. However, if the ghost is a monk, and ghost monks are popular throughout Wessex, that is the only description that is usually offered:

> A ghost of a monk walks from beyond Sturminster Castle to the mill on a certain night of the year.

> There is the ghost of a monk that walks between Milton Abbey and Delcombe Manor.

Sometimes the story is told with more detail, like this one from Perranporth, Cornwall:

> This story is about a hotel that the informant and her husband used to manage in Cornwall. The building used to be a monastery. One night early in the year, she and her husband were going through the building to go to the office to get some envelopes. They had seen in a long passage a figure run from one of the rooms and up the stairs. They gave chase, but found no sign of him, nor was there any way in which he could have entered the place. He wore a long dark coat or mac.

Sometimes the tales of explanation for the ghost are quite old, and tell of strange and often pathetic circumstances. The following tradition told of a ghost at Broad Oak, Sturminster Newton:

The informant had heard of the ghost of Broad Oak, and said that it was a previous owner of the house who had lost all his money by gambling. He was heavily in debt. His wife became tired of being pressed by his creditors, and because she liked to live in luxury left him and went to live with another man. Eventually his house was taken from him, and he died in a debtors' prison. His spirit returned to haunt the house, and it is said that it will continue to do so until the house returns to one of his descendants. This is not very likely, as all his relatives left the district over a hundred years ago.

Bitterness or untimely death are recurrent themes in these tales. Another tale from nearby has a wealth of detail:

A house in Sturminster that was burnt down in the fire of 1729 was said to be haunted by a follower of the Devil, who on the third night of every second month carried a candle into the porch and left it to burn all night. When this man was alive he had lost his wife and three children all within three months, and this had turned him into a bitter recluse. People believed that he worshipped the Devil, and that he could often be seen walking about the house silently carrying the candle. After he had died three families in succession moved into the house, but each left as they were troubled by the strange appearance of this candle, and by the stories that were told by people who believed in this ghost. It is said that after the house was burnt down, and lay in shambles, a candle stood burning in the place where the porch had been, and could not be extinguished until it had burnt itself out.

The detail of this story is unusual, as is its age, for it may date from well before the beginning of the eighteenth century.

Sixteen ghost stories of this general sort were collected in the survey from areas of southern Somerset. Many showed considerable narrative interest and detail. Once again themes of untimely or unhappy death were apparent. The first example is from Cricket Malherbie, near Ilminster.

Someone put up a cross there, and there is supposed to be someone who comes there; it is thought to be the ghost of a young man. He came from Cricket St Thomas, and was in love with

a girl who lived at Cricket Court. He used to walk across White
Down to see her, and then down to the cross. Two brothers
went out one night to meet him, and slew him and buried him
at Cricket Cross. He is supposed to come there.

This tale is a very old one, containing the international theme
of the jealous brothers and the unfortunate lover. Some intrigue
is found in another ghost story from Cudworth.

The Vicarage is supposed to be haunted by the ghost of a man
who died in strange circumstances. He is supposed to have been
pushed down the stairs by his brother [sometimes 'son'] and
thus killed. The present rector, soon after he came to the place,
heard a tumbling noise in a part of the house, and thought that
it was his mother who had fallen down the stairs. However, the
noise came from a different part of the house from that where
the stairs were situated, and his mother was found to be quite
unhurt, and had not in fact tumbled down the stairs. However,
when he did at last locate the spot where the noise came from,
he found that there had at one time been a stairway there, but
it had been removed by a previous owner of the house.

Ghosts as men were also reported from Windwhistle, where they
were highwaymen on horseback, or from Purtington, where
again they were highwaymen but they tapped on the windows
at night as they rode up through the village. There is a strong
tradition of a male ghost at Wake Hill above Ilminster and at
the spot called Chink, mentioned in the previous chapter. The
poltergeist at Chink has received some attention, but an earlier
tradition from there tells of a male ghost, a former landowner
called Monsorel, who after an agreement with an abbot with-
held payment for the land of a pound of wax, and as a result
of his wickedness haunts the spot. We know that a Monsorel
held Dillington in the thirteenth century, and if the tradition
refers to the same man, this particular ghost is old indeed. The
poltergeist now operates on the same spot, and Monsorel seems
to have lost popularity. Immediately above this location on the
road to Dowlish Wake, at a place popularly called Black Gates,
there are numerous traditions; they result in part from the close
proximity of Chink, in part from the isolated and eerie nature

of the spot, and in part from association with the suicide of a former vicar of Dowlish Wake, B. Speke, who lived close by. In one collected version of the story the ghost is in fact a parson, but has acquired the name of Speke's successor, F. M. Mules.

A charming story from Dorset shows not only the theme of murder establishing a ghost, but also that iron is a powerful agent when used against spirits:

> Some time ago, during the last century, a farmer was murdered at the four cross-roads of Gains Cross. The ghost of the man was said to have been seen very often sitting on the gate, near to where the murder took place. This gate fell into disrepair, but no man dared to repair it for fear of angering the ghost. In late years the gate has been replaced, and replaced by an iron one, which according to one informant was too cold for the ghost to sit on.

*J.11.iv. Ghosts as women*

Popular tradition offered as many ghosts of women as of men, though not as many ghost nuns as ghost monks. From Sturminster Newton, Dorset, came a story presenting an interesting parallel to the one given above about a man who was supposed to have sold himself to the Devil:

> This story concerns a house in Sturminster that was destroyed by the fire of 1729. It was haunted by the ghost of a woman who died there. She returned to haunt her husband. On their wedding anniversary every year she could be seen walking upstairs to his room carrying a candle, which she placed outside his door before she entered. It so happened that the day that the house burnt down was the day of their wedding anniversary, and the woman's husband was found dead in his bed with the candle burning outside the door. He did not die of burns, and the candle could not be extinguished until he was buried beside his wife, and then it went out of its own accord.

There appears to be some trace of the belief of the transmigration of the soul here. This story and the one similar to it were told by the same informant. There is no doubt certain confusion in transmission, and parts of one tale have become intermixed with another; it is likely that originally there were two completely different stories.

Female ghosts are often uncanny and not altogether pleasant. On the road from Almer to Wareham near the World's End Inn can be seen the ghost of a woman who warns of an imminent death in the Wells family. Tradition tells that she was badly treated by the family and takes her revenge whenever she can. The ghost of a witch is supposed to appear at Charlton Marshall on Hallowe'en night. In some cases the ghost is mounted, often on a white horse: a woman rides through the road tunnel near Beaminster on a horse, and near Corfe, Somerset, the ghost of a lady on a white horse passes through a gate without opening it or jumping over it, and rides across the field to disappear into the earth; this ghost story is almost certainly a remnant of fairy lore. The Green Lady of Crowcombe warns of coming illness, and similar apparitions have been reported from Somerton and Holcombe (Mendips). The Green Lady is a very unlucky ghost to see indeed, and is an Other World fairy creature that has passed into oral tradition as a ghost. The White Ghost seen in the grounds of Bryanston House, Dorset, warned of the death of one of the family who lived in the old house, though some say that she is the ghost of a woman who committed suicide on her wedding day by throwing herself off the church tower. Pimperne Rectory is supposed to be haunted by the ghost of one of the wives of Henry VIII, and in some versions she walks about without her head. The manor of Pimperne was granted for life by Henry VIII to Queen Catherine Howard, and three years later to Queen Catherine Parr. At the latter's death it was granted by Elizabeth to William Tooke and Edward Baesh. The rectory was a different building from the manor, the former being rebuilt at the beginning of the eighteenth century. But Queen Catherine is named as a patron of the rectors of Pimperne from 1509–36, and Queen Jane from 1536–1682, patronage extending beyond the death, with the life of the incumbent. This is the connection with Henry VIII that has given rise to the story; it is not likely that any wife of Henry visited the place. Anne Boleyn is said to ride round Aylsham, Norfolk, in a black coach, with black headless horses and headless coachman. The body lights the interior of the coach with a red glow, and the journey ends at Blicking Hall.

### *J.11.v. Headless body*

Whether this motif has any connection with primitive lore related to beheading and the laying of spirits it is hard to say. It seems to be just a popular macabre decoration, adding descriptive force to an existing longer tale.

> In a very hard winter someone was walking to Crewkerne, and they had to walk on the top of the hedgerows, as the snow was so deep. He saw something strange, and they told him that it was the ghost of a headless man, evidently from the time when the highwaymen were wild up there.

The informant who gave this tale from Windwhistle, Somerset, explained that she thought she had read the story somewhere many years before. We know its literary source, though the author most probably extracted it from oral tradition at the time.[4] The event involves the chase across Windwhistle of a smuggler and a coastguard on a snowy night in the time of George II. It resulted in much bloodshed and is still vaguely remembered in oral tradition in the area. Indeed, the lore of ghosts, phantom horse-riders and sounds of galloping is common round there. The informant above has supplied a headless man who was never in the original, but augments an otherwise scanty story.

Numerous other headless ghosts were reported. One walks up the hill from Blandord Forum towards Wimborne, while Somerset provided similar stories from Bickenhall, Corfe and Churchstanton, though in each of these cases the ghost was mounted on a horse.

### *J.11.vi. Spectral coaches*

Many stories of phantom coaches, with horses and drivers often headless, were found in the Dorset area, most being associated with country houses, or old coach roads where coaches would have been seen. The memory of their existence has passed down as a haunting, and may well be compared with the belief held in some places that a ghost train may be heard, or even seen, travelling along a now disused railway line. In Somerset a phantom coach was reported from Windwhistle, where the driver had no head, since it had been cut off by highwaymen. Another followed the old road down through Hinton Park to Hinton House. In Dorset ten stories were collected, most of them telling of a phantom coach that was to be seen at certain locations between Langton House, Blandford Forum and Tarrant Gunville.

> A coach and four, with a coachman in old-fashioned dress, has been seen going past Langton Church.

> Near Ashley Wood Golf Course there is a turning to Langton, and many people have heard the sound of galloping horses and a carriage, but as the sound came nearer they realised that there was no horse and carriage.

> There is a ghostly carriage with a headless driver that comes over the down to Tarrant Gunville, and up the drive to Eastbury House. After a few minutes it comes down the drive again and carries on up the road to Stubhampton. Quite some time ago blue ribbons were found on one of the tombs in the churchyard. These were thought to be the driver's garters.

There were several other stories, but all showed a feasible geographical continuity: a phantom coach and horses is seen and heard along its route by different people who have no knowledge of its total extent. The two houses of Eastbury and Langton were at one stage owned by the same family, the former being purchased by the Farquharsons in 1806, the latter being built for James John Farquharson in the period before the accession of Queen Victoria.

### J.11.vii. Spectral funerals

Headless men are also found in traditions concerning the spectral funeral. Four such men carry a coffin along one of the roads from Lytchett to Poole for some distance, and finally disappear into a hedge. There is supposed to be a spectral funeral at a place called Four Lanes, below Chilworth in Somerset, and another at Wood Court tells of a procession that passes diagonally across the field in front of the court and into the old chapel. On the road between Roadwater and Golsoncott near Washford, a hearse was supposed to cross the road at right angles and disappear.

*J.12. Specific ghosts known by name*
The ghost tradition is often seen at its best in stories about a specific ghost whose name is known. Details of the incidents surrounding the story are usually included. The Grey Lady group of ghosts may be dealt with here. The Grey Lady is a ghost frequently encountered in older country houses; she appears from time to time, and frequently as a warning that a death is imminent. Keynston Lodge, Dorset, is supposed to have a Grey Lady, though in the tradition collected she did not appear as a death warning. Hinton House has a Grey Lady, although traditions in the area also call her simply a ghost, while Whitestaunton Manor House has a more specific tradition:

> There was a story of a monk who murdered a woman on the steps going up to the well. The ghost of the murdered lady was called the Grey Lady. There seemed to be considerable suspicion about the Grey Lady, as she was said to haunt the house, and the area around it. Some said that she haunted the copse nearby, which is called the Royal Copse.

Several versions of the tradition were collected. At Loe, near Launceston, a Grey Lady would appear in a certain room of a big old house, now a hotel, when someone was about to die. The story has filtered into literary tradition, and we find it in Henry James's *The Portrait of a Lady*.[5]
Other named ghosts are more dramatic. Wake Hill, Somerset, has already been mentioned in some detail. There follows a

radition told with some enthusiasm that begins with a ghost
f a parson encountered at this place:

> May was coming up from Ilminster with a friend, and they saw
> this ghost come up. It touched her on the left arm. She told her
> friend Amy to turn round and look, but told her not to put her
> torch on, or else it would disappear. She turned round and saw
> it. He was tall and dark and did not look very pleasant. This was
> the ghost of Parson Mules.
> There was another ghost down in Dowlish Church. Amy
> Miller's mother used to clean the church. She saw old Mr
> Braughton coming from the vestry, and come and sit down in
> his own seat—because they all had their own seats. She said,
> 'Alright, Mr Braughton, I ain't going to hurt 'ee.' He was from
> Manor Farm. Parson Mules was a ghost because he had drowned
> himself in the tank.

he confusion between Mules and B. Speke has been com-
nented upon previously. From Broadway comes this story
bout Jack Robinson:

> Somerset Cottage was haunted by Jack Robinson. It was once
> a relay station on the main road. Someone from Broadway saw
> the ghost while ill in bed there. The origin of the saying 'Jack
> Robinson' comes from here.

rief though it is, the story is worthy of comment for two
easons. First, we can date it, as Jack Robinson did exist, and
econdly it is a good example of the folk explanation for a
opular saying. Robinson was the keeper of two extra horses
hat were used to tug carriages and waggons up Buckland Hill;
s horses were replaced he lost his job. He seems to have been
 rather eccentric character living finally on ' "tatur parings"
 .rnips and the like, till well nigh starved',[6] until he was lured
 ) Chard workhouse. The phrase 'Jack Robinson' dates back
 t least to the eighteenth century, and certainly did not
 riginate here.[7]
A famous named ghost in Somerset is that of Popham, who
ccording to tradition was killed while hunting—he fell into a
ool, and was drowned. Because of the pious prayers of his

wife, however, his spirit was able to proceed to its rest by one cock's stride a year, to reach Wellington Church. His ghost still haunts the area round Hemyock. In fact Popham died on 1 June 1607, being struck with a fatal disease at the age of seventy-two. He was buried in the parish church of St John the Baptist at Wellington, where the south chancel aisle contains an elaborate tomb. How tradition assigns his death to a hunting accident in Wilscombe Bottom I cannot imagine, except that he was almost universally detested by the people of Somerset, a distinction he shares with Judge Jeffreys. It was the transaction over the Littlecote estates that seems to have brought him most into disrepute, though the stories of his childhood did him little credit. Miss Tongue gave me this:

> There is a memory of Sydenham riding down the Monksilver road, because of what he did. He was a very bad man. He and Popham connived to get hold of the lands of Littlecote. By a legal trick Popham got the lands, and Sydenham got the cash. This is still remembered by the folk.

There is no historical evidence to support the statement that Sydenham was in any way implicated in the affair over the Littlecote estates. George Sydenham would have been a contemporary of Popham, and could have known him, but otherwise the tale is without foundation.

Eastbury House in Dorset has a tradition about the ghost of a butler who shot himself; there is supposed to be a blood stain in the room concerned that cannot be removed. A house at Hambrook, Gloucestershire, also has an unmovable blood stain where someone was murdered. At Eastbury I have heard it said that at certain times the whole of the front of the house runs with blood:

> The master of the house was lost while crossing the Red Sea, and was believed to be dead. For some reason part of the house was pulled down, but the message was received that the master was safe and well, and was on his way home. At this news the butler shot himself, and his ghost still walks in the servants' quarters.

Other versions have it that the butler was stabbed and that he drips blood as he walks. The house, designed by Sir John Vanbrugh in 1718, was originally very large, being exceeded in size only by Blenheim and Castle Howard. It took over twenty years to build. On the owner's death in 1770 it passed to George Bubb, who in turn passed it to a nephew who offered £200 to any gentleman who would look after the place. As there were no offers most of the house was pulled down, one wing being converted into a smaller house that is still inhabited. The Farquharsons bought Eastbury in 1806. The butler story quoted above has some measure of fact behind it, and the house has always been the subject of some mystery. The butler seems in some way responsible for the pulling down of the house, and has become the folk's explanation for the deed. The present owner of the house told me that in fact there was a butler who shot himself in the building while his master was away.

The Monk of Shaftesbury is another well-known ghost of Wessex. The monk is supposed to have been ordered by the abbess to secure a hiding place for the gold and silver of the church, as Henry VIII's men were on their way. The monk employed a blind old workman who could not speak to construct a safe place for the treasure. On his way back to the abbess he had a heart attack and died, and with him died the secret of where the treasure was hidden. He is to be seen in a brown habit along Abbey Walk, and disappears through the wall where presumably there was a door. He is only visible from the knees upwards. Excavations made in 1932 failed to uncover the secret. The plate from the abbey was never discovered, and the ghost is truly a treasure guardian, most probably dating in oral tradition from the sixteenth century—the dissolution took place here on 2 March 1539.

Tom Dewfall's ghost from Sturminster Newton is interesting as an example of how traditions become updated.

> A woman in Sturminster saw a man whom she recognised as a friend whom she had not seen for many years. His name was Thomas Dewfall. As she went to speak to him, he signalled to her not to speak but he walked with her. They passed a house

K

where the women left him to tell the occupant of Tom's arrival, as he was also a friend of his. On leaving the house, the woman found that Tom had gone, but attached little importance to it. The next day on passing the same house the woman called in to see her friend, and was told that news had just come that Tom had died shortly before the woman had seen him.

During the First World War a number of children from Blandford Grammar School were to be evacuated to America on the *Lusitania*. The night before the ship set sail, the parents of one of the girls who was to leave both had a frightening nightmare. The girl's mother was the daughter of the woman who had been with Tom Dewfall the morning he died.

In the nightmare the couple dreamed that they saw Tom Dewfall in a very distressed state, wringing his hands, and shaking his head. On waking, the couple decided that Tom was giving them warning of somebody's death, and they did not allow their daughter to sail on the *Lusitania*. The *Lusitania* was later torpedoed and most of the passengers and crew perished.

The dream-warning theme is found frequently, though the confusions in this story have developed in part from oral transmission and partly, I suspect, because the tale is to be found in O. Knott's *Old Dorset* (Poole, 1958), pp 53–5. Though Knott gives some additional material not in the example above, the confusion may well result from her statement that the dream incident took place during World War I, naming the ship as the *Lusitania*. In fact this ship was sunk in 1915, being responsible for bringing the Americans into the war against Germany; in any case, it was on its way from America to England. The evacuation part of the story is even more suspect. Perhaps the event concerned the *Athenia*, sunk in 1939 while taking 1,416 men, women and children to America—112 lives were lost.[8] However, the ship was outward bound from Liverpool, not Southampton. The tradition shows the usual confusion and mixture of fact and fiction.

Winterborne Stickland has the ghost of Mr Skinner in its church. A ghost is essentially a pagan object, and its presence in a holy building is always interesting:

Mr Skinner haunts the church at Stickland, but no one seems to know why, as there do not seem to be any unusual circumstances about his death. He has been seen by different reliable people on many occasions. One time he knocked some books off the altar. When they were picked up there was a pool of blood on the floor. He was seen one night during a power cut by the choir and congregation at Evensong. He appeared to walk across from the Skinner Chapel to the altar and look at the congregation. Perhaps he was used to having his rest disturbed at the same time on Sunday, and wondered what the sudden darkness was for. The previous rector, Canon Low, is reputed to have seen him many times in the church, and was firmly convinced that there was a ghost. At Hallowe'en this year [1969] vandals got into the Skinner Chapel, and tried to remove the top of the tomb. After this Mr Skinner was seen several times during the week.

Mr Skinner died on 5 October 1756 aged sixty-eight, and was buried on the 13th of same month. His wife died in 1769, leaving £200 to provide bread for the poor of the parish. Skinner's tomb is in the Skinner Chapel, and is a large, impressive, marble-topped construction, though it is probable that he is buried in his vault beneath the church.

A ghost story collected in 1969 from Wyke Regis in Dorset can only be a few years old, and tells of the sergeant from Glasgow. The tale was supplied by Mr R. W. Patten.

This took place while I was working with the Somerset Army in the kitchen of the Sergeants' Mess. After closing the bar, the Mess was made ready for the next day. One morning, however, when the bar was opened up, it was found that a table had been moved, a big cup knocked over and other cups moved, but nothing was missing. Since the place was a bar, and the takings were kept there, the room was securely locked. None of these locks had been tampered with.

Then one of the locals told me this story:

A few years earlier, the Airborne Division had been stationed there, and one of the sergeants from Glasgow had been well-known for his high spirits. Soon afterwards the Airborne Division had been moved to Aden, and this particular sergeant was killed. It was believed he was killed by a stray bullet from behind his own lines.

The division returned to the camp, and one night there were three sergeants sleeping in the Mess, as all the others were out on an exercise. One of the three awoke and saw someone leaning over a table. He shouted and woke the other two, and they all saw this person fade away and claimed that it was the sergeant who had been shot in Aden.

The details about the room not having been tampered with by normal agencies and the somewhat unnatural death of the sergeant are typical of a tale in the process of becoming adopted into oral tradition.

### *J.15. Serpents and dragons*

There are several dragon legends recorded in Wessex, though most of these have now gone from oral tradition. Swamp dragons are recorded from Ker Moor, near Dunster, where St Carantoc captured a huge serpent that roamed the moor by throwing his cloak over it. He took it to the king at Dunster Castle who inspected it. The saint fed the monster and then let it go, telling it to do no more harm. The Aller dragon came out of the Athelney fens, and was killed by an Aller man with a 9ft long javelin. At Norton Fitzwarren a dragon grew out of a pile of corpses left after a battle in which the British inhabitants of Norton Fitzwarren camp were slaughtered. It ravaged the countryside and was killed by Fulk Fitzwarine, who also killed the Kingston Dragon. The latter tale seems to be an extension of the Norton tradition.[9] The very fine screen carvings in Norton Fitzwarren Church show that local craftsmen were at least familiar with the tradition, as does the fine bench-end in Crowcombe Church that shows a two-headed dragon being attacked by a group of men. Both carvings probably date from the end of the fifteenth century. Miss Tongue tells a dragon story from Shervage Wood.[10]

None of these dragons are treasure guardians, but it has been suggested that their memory in folk tradition stems from the invasions of the Danes (see J.11.i). The Danes used the dragon as decoration for their standards. Both Norton camp and Dowsborough camp were probably attacked by the Danes, though the dragons of Aller and Ker Moor certainly belong to a different tradition.

Miss Tongue told me a story about a treasure-guarding dragon at Castle Neroche, that bore a remarkable resemblance to her 'Dene Hole Dragon', as given in *Forgotten Folk Tales of the English Counties* (1970), p 5. Castle Neroche is medieval, not suiting a Scandinavian treasure-guardian, and the similarity of the two stories leads one to the conclusion that the placing of a dragon there results from some confusion.

### J.17. Hidden treasure

Stories about hidden treasure never quite lose their fascination; there is always the feeling that these stories just might be true. The slightest chance of gaining sudden wealth will always excite interest. By analogy no doubt with genuine finds, burial mounds are often associated with traditions of buried treasure:

> There are some burial mounds in a field by the road from Bere Regis to Wimborne. It is said that there is treasure buried in these mounds.

Usually the penalty for removing the treasure is extreme, as it involves interference with the supernatural world, a condition that has already been examined. Traditions fall into several categories, but chiefly consist of those that simply state that there is treasure buried at a certain place, and those that record the adventures of people who have tried to dig it out.

To the former belong such plain statements as this one from Dorset:

> There is a legend of a silver table that is said to be buried under some yew trees about half a mile from the village.
>
> (Tarrant Gunville)

Another, more detailed story about a table was found at Hilcombe, near Ilminster. The well mentioned was near the site of an old house that fell into disuse or was destroyed by fire sometime after 1700.

> There was a well there in which there was a golden table. It was put there by the German occupants just before the war. People with chains tried to haul it up, but it always fell back just before it reached the surface.

Which war is meant is not clear, though this may be a case where the informant has updated the story. In another version the table is silver and involves a speaking taboo:

> This happened after the Reformation, or something, when 'they' were coming. There is now a well there in which there is a silver table, taken from the house, which is no longer there. The story goes that people tried to take it up, but if anyone spoke as they tried to pull it up, it fell back again.

A further version suggested that a table and 'things' were left in the well and that the table had a silver top. The story is an old one, and probably older than the destruction of the house. The place was a 'seat of a knight' in 1690, and cottage stone nearby, which was probably taken from the old house, is dated 1705. The owner of the house at the time of the Civil War was a Royalist called Sir Edward Berkeley who was 'in consequence thereof . . . mulcted in £100 on his "Manor of Hilcombe Wall" '.[11] The tradition may well date from this time.

Treasure is sometimes guarded by a ghost who may go off and find rest at last when he has shown a human being where it is hidden. The Monk of Shaftesbury is one such ghost. There was another at Merriott, Somerset, who was supposed to appear at a big house there. Someone rebuilt one of the walls in the house, and there found a great sum of money which was used to build the Wesleyan Chapel. After this the ghost was no longer seen. In Blandford Forum, Dorset, a tradition is told about a baker who had fallen on hard times and had to work late into the night. One night a little old lady came to him, and asking him why he worked so late showed him a certain place in the garden, and told him to dig there next day. This he did, and there found a large sum of money that set him on his feet again. At Sea near Ilminster, Somerset, there is supposed to be a ghost who, if followed, will take you to a large quantity of money. There is supposed to be hidden wealth at Cudworth and at Wood Court—both places mentioned before in other connections. The former gave a tradition with another speaking taboo:

> In a field there is a moat and earthworks. In a dip, nine to ten feet across, there is supposed to be some buried treasure put there by the monks or knights. No one has been able to dig it up. The last fellow who tried got down so far, and the whole lot fell in on top of him. No one tried to dig him out, but it was filled in on top of him.

The unlucky aspect of treasure-digging is established in the stories told about standing stones. The stone at Culm Davy is supposed to have money buried beneath it, but no one has been able to move it; the same is said of the one at Staple Fitzpaine:

> They used to reckon that a fellow named Crandon, a relation to the one who lives up there now, hid his money underneath the stone. Some fellows decided to move the stone. One of them said that they must say nothing. They heaved and one said, 'Damn thing isn't going.' After this they had no chance of moving it because one of them had sworn.

In this case the failure was caused by blasphemy, indicating that the stone or whatever could only be manipulated by help from above, though purer versions are most probably simple speaking taboos; to speak while pulling something from the clutches of the supernatural would awake the spirits to the presence of humans and so spoil the spell. While haymaking in the early summer of 1970 in Dorset, I uttered an oath of the sort not uncommon when bales are heavy and have to be lifted high, and a local worker said 'You'll never lift 'e if 'e talk that way.'

Castle Neroche provides some of the most detailed and interesting stories about buried treasure and the adventures of treasure diggers. This is an example of a man-made mound that was never, as far as we know, a burial mound; it became, according to tradition, both hollow and filled with treasure. The digs that have actually taken place may originally have been to seek for treasure, but more likely, and certainly more recently, they have been for archaeological reasons. Nevertheless, folk traditions provide an interesting collection of stories based on these digs, crediting the diggers with gold fever, and punishing most of them for their avarice.

The tradition in its simple form usually runs like this:

> Legend says that there is treasure in Castle Neroche mound. Forty or fifty years ago six local people started to dig for treasure. They dug from the top, and the digging became very hard work. The diggers got annoyed and blasphemed. At once the hole closed in on top of them, half burying them.

With a little expansion the tradition develops more story:

> There were in fact two digs into the mound for treasure. The first time there was thunder at the end, and ill fortune followed those who dug. On the second occasion however they found a great box. One of them blasphemed in surprise and the box slipped from his grasp into the sand and was never seen again.

Some informants were less imaginative, and merely said that attempts had failed because of lack of funds, or because of loss of interest, but a literary source told very graphically how the men had dug into the mound and found the trunk, but had sworn, and caused the trunk to slip from view—and worse than that, the sides of the hole had then closed in on top of them and it was all they could do to escape. After that ill-fortune dogged them all. The work went on, but one broke his leg, and another crushed his foot. Finally a very sultry air fell on the place, and a great thunderstorm broke over them, which was too much for them; they all fled, convinced that the Devil was up there.[12]

From the historical point of view the first dig into the mound seems to have been made about two hundred years ago by some men from Corfe, and this is the one that seems to have caught the imagination of the people. The Rev F. Warre gave a more or less full account of it in 1854, and leaves little doubt as to his opinion of it:

> I have now only to draw attention to the deep indentations on the side of the beacon. These are modern ravages, and their

true history is as follows. About a hundred years ago, a number of labouring men, urged on by the love of filthy lucre and not having the fear of archaeological societies before their eyes . . . with sacriligious spade and pick axe violated the sanctity of this mysterious hill. But before they had found a single coin they were seized with a panic fear, renounced their presumptuous enterprise and, wonderful and awful to relate, within one month of the commencement of their enterprise, some by accident, some by sudden death, and some by violent fevers, all paid with their lives the penalty of their covetous and most presumptuous attempt. Oh! that this most veracious legend were universally published as a warning to all wanton mutilators of ancient earthworks.[13]

The author was the man responsible for the first dig into the mound that was archaeologically orientated, but he left no real record of his finds, and his theories were later proved to be false. A more scientific dig was conducted by Hinton St George Gray in 1903, and the most recent excavations took place in 1962, the report of which has still to be published. None of these later digs seem to have encountered any difficulties of the sort experienced by the men from Corfe.

### *J.18.iii. Supernatural objects*

Some objects are credited with supernatural powers. A famous example from the area of this study is the Combe Sydenham cannon-ball:

> In a big house at this place there was a large ball by the table leg. People had been known to take it away, but somehow it always got back to the house before the person who took it away returned themselves.

Miss Tongue gave me a fuller version:

> The cannon ball was in fact a meteorite. When Drake was off round the world he was to have married Elizabeth Sydenham. However, her father found her a better suitor. But Drake was a wizard, and he sent a cannon ball from the other side of the world, that landed in front of the bridal party, and so stopped

the wedding. The ball is supposed to roll in times of national disaster, and return to the house of its own accord if taken away.

The Sydenham family lived at Combe Sydenham since the fourteenth century. The house was sold in 1730 to the Musgroves. The 'cannon-ball' or the object that was supposed to be one was in Taunton Museum, though it is doubtful if in fact it was a meteorite. Drake was regarded as a wizard both in popular Somerset and Devon tradition, and by the French. He married the only surviving daughter of Sir George Sydenham, from which event the story obviously comes. The tale is well known, and in one other recorded version the cannon-ball rolled into the house where it has stayed ever since.[14] Drake produced a fleet to sail against the Armada by whittling a stick into the English Channel; as each piece of stick touched the water, it sprang up as a ship.

# CHAPTER 11

# HISTORICAL TRADITIONS

Properly, many of the traditions considered in this chapter are legends. Their interest in a study of oral tradition is twofold: they often provide a strong narrative, lacking in the shorter myths; and where a story is based on an actual historical incident, the full process of transmutation may be seen by comparing it with a study of the documented incident.

*K.1. Individual personages*
The best known individual found in traditions told in Wessex is King Arthur. Oral tradition about the king is less fanciful than the literary counterparts. Often it is difficult to establish whether the literary source came first and then passed into oral tradition, or vice versa. Many localities that claim a connection with Arthur probably did so long before most of the written

stories, for which authors added material from the continent, producing romances such as *Historia Regum Britanniae* written in the early twelfth century by Geoffrey of Monmouth. Geoffrey used a ninth-century work by Nennius, the first writer to mention Arthur, and a book now lost but lent to him by the Archdeacon of Oxford. Layamon's *Brut* added much to the story, including the fairies at Arthur's birth and his journey to Avalon, as well as Sir Gawain and Sir Bedivere. The subject was much used on the other side of the Channel as well, and later taken up by Thomas Malory and eventually by Tennyson in his *Idylls of the King*.

There is some case for supposing that Henry I encouraged Geoffrey of Monmouth to establish Arthur as a national hero. The popular association of Arthur with Glastonbury may have arisen for similar reasons, though whether there was a tradition concerning Arthur and Glastonbury before the time of its exploitation is unfortunately not known. Arthur was supposed to have been buried at Glastonbury, perhaps by association with the name itself, or because it was said that he descended on his mother's side from Joseph of Arimathea (see Chapter 7). It was said that the tomb of Arthur was found at Glastonbury in the reign of Henry II. It was 16ft deep, and was located between two pillars. The coffin was of oak or elder, and an inscription on a leaden cross was found above the coffin. It read:

> Hic jacet Arthurus, Rex quondam,
> Rexque futurus.

As a writer has commented, 'There is almost every reason to believe that this extraordinary "find" could be nothing but a pious fraud, "in majorem monasterii gloriam".'[1]

The Arthur of oral tradition bears little resemblance to the king and his Round Table of the romances. No doubt some stories of Arthur were at one time wholly in oral tradition, but one suspects that in the case of a place such as Glastonbury the effect of the romances on oral tradition has been greater than the effect of oral tradition on the romances. Arthur is popularly associated with many other places throughout Wessex. One of his traditional birthplaces was of course Tintagel, Cornwall, though at South Cadbury is the true Camelot, according to Leyland. A causeway extending across the lowland to the north of the hill is known as King Arthur's Causeway, along which the king used to ride to pay homage to the abbot at Glastonbury. Some say that the hill is full of treasure, while others say that the Cadbury Hill near Nailsea was Camelot, that Arthur and his knights still sleep beneath it, and that if you could find the right entrance you would see them there; if you shouted they would wake and ride out once more. This tradition is similar to others found in the north of England and in Wales. In Dorset Arthur is sometimes associated with Badbury Rings, though little narrative tradition has been collected about the legend.

### K.5.iii. The Romans

The Romans become associated in folk tradition with all sorts of remains, frequently with little justification. No doubt false scholarship is sometimes to blame, as with Castle Neroche, Somerset:

> Legend has it that the camp was originally Roman, and that it had a moat around it, and it was a sort of castle.

> Castle Neroche was of course Roman, and there was a Roman road from Taunton to Bathpool.

The results of excavations are sometimes referred to:

> Castle Neroche was supposed to be Roman, but the informant was not sure about this. There were a great many things dug out of there when the informant was a little girl, many old Roman things.

This location and its history was discussed in the last chapters. Other traditional assumptions have more reason behind them. At Wadeford, near Chard, are the remains of a Roman villa. By association with this an informant supplied the following:

> Behind the Co-op in Wadeford there was supposed to be a Roman churchyard. Once they had foot and mouth disease,

and the Italians were there, and someone said, 'That's where your Roman forebears are buried.'

Only a villa has been excavated at Wadeford, and there is no evidence to prove the existence of a burial ground. Similarly, by analogy with the remains of a Roman villa at Whitestaunton, one informant told me that the manor house there was Roman. The Roman villa is sited in the grounds of the house, which in fact dates from the fifteenth century, and was much enlarged by the Bretts in Elizabethan times.

The Romans are also associated with Lulworth Cove in Dorset. There is a tradition that they used to bring their elephants there to train on the slopes. This unusual story is probably an extension of the larger body of lore that tells of the ghosts of a Roman army that can be heard and sometimes seen marching over the Purbecks above Lulworth. Similarly the ghost of a Roman centurion is said to haunt both Hod and Hambledon Hills, though these stories belong with ghost lore and are not true historical traditions.

*K.5.vi. Civil War*

The Civil War is remembered in Wessex, though most of the traditions have become confused with a more important event for the area, the Monmouth rebellion. Thus the tree at Whitelackington near Ilminster that is variously described as an oak or a chestnut becomes associated with Cromwell, whereas in fact it was a sweet chestnut associated with Monmouth. One informant claimed that there was a Cromwell tree in the garden of the vicarage at Broadway, while another claimed that Wellington or Monmouth hid in the farmhouse on Castle Neroche. Such comments are the result of false history, but throughout the historical traditions there seems to be a delight in the perpetuation of inaccurate statements, the original being often far less exciting. Fight Ground, near Barrington Hill, Somerset, is also erroneously associated with the Civil War:

> There was supposed to have been a battle there years ago. It was said to have been in Cromwell's time. There is a little lane

and a little drove opposite; this is called Oliver's Lane, and would lead right up to Fight Ground. It dates from Oliver Cromwell.

n fact the name dates from Monmouth's time, when a skirmish ook place there between Monmouth's rebels and Churchill's couts. A weapon was dug up there at about the turn of the entury. The Royalists lost one man and Monmouth four, and everal were wounded.

In Dorset the Civil War has left more of a mark. The Dorset men, tired of the Civil War, set up in opposition against all comers on Hambledon Hill, and held out until defeated by Cromwell in 1645. Parliamentary armies marched through Blandford Forum in 1643 and 1644. The town was taken by the Royalists but recaptured by the Parliamentarians and given up for plunder. From this time dates a tradition resulting from a skirmish:

Pimperne was near to a spot where there was a skirmish between Roundheads and Cavaliers. The people of Pimperne captured one whom they opposed, and cut his hand off as a punishment. When the punished man's side took the village they buried the hand in the proper manner, presumably in the churchyard.

In some versions of the story the hand haunts the grave at Pimperne. In other versions the hand was severed in a dispute resulting from poachers being attacked by keepers. This was the Battle of Chettle Common, 16 December 1780. The man who lost the hand was a trumpet major from Blandford. The hand was said to have been buried at Pimperne, though sometimes it is supposed to haunt the Bloody Shard Gate at Tarrant Gunville, not far from Chettle Common. Oral tradition seems to have either updated an event by over a hundred years, or more likely confused an event from the Civil War with a deerstealing tradition.

### K.5.vii. Monmouth and Judge Jeffreys

The events of the Monmouth rebellion are still well remembered in Wessex, and in particular in Somerset. As with some of the historical traditions already discussed many of the stories told were inaccurate but well maintained. The traditions concern two main areas: first, Monmouth and the rebellion itself, and secondly Judge Jeffreys and the Bloody Assize.

James Monmouth was born at Rotterdam, the son of Lucy Walter—by Charles II, it was claimed, but more likely by Colonel Robert Sidney. James came to England in 1662, and in the following year was created Duke of Monmouth. He became increasingly popular, though in fact he seems to have been a rather weak character, and he cultivated his popularity by two semi-royal progresses (1680-2). It was during one of these progresses that he first came to Somerset:

> Monmouth used to ride quite often up through Moolham to visit Speke at Wake Hill, then on through Long Ponds to Whitelackington. This was before Sedgemoor.

The informant was one of the few to establish that the connection of Monmouth with the area was mainly before the rebellion.

> They say that Monmouth stopped at North Lodge, Hinton St George, and there was a feast there.

Monmouth journeyed from Longleat to Whitelackington, where it was computed that 20,000 people greeted him—no doubt a liberal estimate. He went to Barrington Court, Chard, and Forde Abbey, and attended Ilminster Church on Sunday 29 August 1680. He also probably visited Hinton House, where his visit was celebrated by a feast of junket.[2]

It is the association of Monmouth with Whitelackington that is significant here. The owner of the house was George Speke who soon after Monmouth's visit was questioned before the king, being a likely perpetrator of sedition. Judge Jeffreys did not like the Spekes, as we shall see later. In 1680 the spectacle at Whitelackington House must have been an unusual one:

> From hence to Mr Speke's in Somersetshire, in which progress he was caressed with the joyful acclamation of the country people . . . within ten miles of Mr Speke's, he was met by 2,000

persons on horseback, whose numbers still increased . . . and when they arrived there, they were reported to be 20,000; wherefore they were forced to break down several pearch of his Park Railes to inlarge their passage to the house, where his Grace and all his numerous company were entertained.[3]

Traditionally Monmouth addressed the people and rested beneath the Monmouth Tree. This is still to be seen in the grounds of the house, and is perhaps 850 years old. While it is unlikely that Monmouth rested there, it is possible that he addressed the crowds beneath it. The tree, a sweet chestnut, was blown down in a storm on Ash Wednesday, 3 March 1897. Its remains are still considerable, but its original dimensions are given as: diameter at foot, 12ft 3in; girth mid-trunk, 25ft; girth top-trunk, 25ft; height from bole to top trunk, 17ft; total height of tree, 49ft. Later Monmouth fled to the Low Countries, having become involved in the Rye House plot. Traditions connecting him with Whitelackington strangely ignore his first and real visit. Rather they connect the place with his flight from Sedgemoor.

The informant said that she had been taught about the tree when she was at school, but had forgotten much. She thought that Monmouth was supposed to have passed the place, and hidden in the oak. He then went into the big house and hid there for the night.

The Duke of Monmouth fled from the battle of Sedgemoor and hid in the tree. It was not known whether he went into the house or not.

In the big house at Whitelackington there is still the rope hanging up where they were going to hang Monmouth. The informant said that she had actually seen it.

Someone hanged themselves at the Manor House at Whitelackington, it was probably the Duke of Monmouth. The informant said that he had seen the rope hanging down in one of the rooms, but he thought that it had probably gone now.

At Charles's death, in concert with Argyll's Scottish expedition, Monmouth landed on 11 June 1685 at Lyme Regis. He

L

collected men for his cause on his way, passed through Axminster and Chard, and reached Ilminster on Wednesday, 17 June. It is said that there he shook hands with one of the Spekes. He may have camped at Winterhay. He then proceeded to Taunton, and ventured towards Bridgwater and Sedgemoor where the last battle to be fought on English soil took place, resulting in his defeat. An account taken from the registers of Weston Zoyland Church gives the best idea of the event:

> An account of the Ffight that was in Langmore, the Six of July, 1685 between the King's Army and the Duke of Monmouth.
>
> The Iniadgement began between one and two of the clock in the morning. It continued near one hour and a halfe. There were killed upon the spott of the King's soldiers, sixteen, ffive of them buried in the Churchyard, and they all had Christian buriall. One hundred or more of the King's soldiers wounded; of which wounds many died, of which we have no certain account. There was kild of the rebels upon the spot about 300; hanged with us 22, of which four were hanged in gemmarek [probably chains]. Aboute 500 prisoners brought into our church, of which there was 79 wounded, and 5 of them died of their wounds in our church.[4]

Monmouth's army was ill-equipped and the venture was doomed from the start. He fled from the field and was discovered hiding in a ditch near Ringwood, dressed as a shepherd, half starving and wretched. He pleaded for his life before James, and even offered to turn Catholic, but was beheaded on Tower Hill on 15 July.

Tradition tells how the scars on one of the buttresses of the church at Weston Zoyland were made by the rebels sharpening their weapons before the battle, though they are more likely to be the result of natural weathering. The image of Christ was said to have been seen moving among the dead and the wounded on the battlefield after the defeat.

The second main element in the Monmouth tradition relates to the Bloody Assize. Once again tradition is often at variance with fact, though Somerset people in particular still tend to feel strongly about the actions of the judge. Jeffreys started on his journey from Winchester in August 1685. He went to Salisbury, and then to Dorchester, where the first real hangings took place. He journeyed to Exeter for the assize of 14 September and then to Taunton, where the assize was held in the Great Hall of the castle. Thence he left for Bristol, leaving on 21 September for Wells. Courts were thus not held locally, but the hangings were, as a warning to others. Just how many people were hanged is not really known. Some found pardon, and others died in prison. According to one authority 233 prisoners were hanged, drawn and quartered. Fifty-four guilty persons were from Ilminster, some of whom did find pardon.[5] However, a list published in 1686 gives ninety-seven to be executed, and many more reprieved, though there are none mentioned as coming from Ilminster. Whatever was the true number, and it seems to have been over a hundred, the public execution of so many locals, some of them of no little standing, and the barbarous custom of hanging, drawing and quartering, aroused a resentment and hatred of the judge that is still found today. An account of the executions at Weymouth gives some idea of the spectacle that most towns and villages in the region must have witnessed:

To a bill of disbursem$^{ts}$ for ye gallows.
Burning and boyling ye Rebells executed, p. order att this towne £16 4s 3d.
Nov. 20 pd. M$^r$ Mayor all ye beare for so much he pd for new setting up a post w$^{th}$ the quart$^{rs}$ of ye Rebells att Waym$^s$ Towne End as p. his bill 1s 6d.[6]

Although the assize was held at several main centres, tradition associates many old houses and buildings with the judge, for inexplicable reasons. It is a common tradition to hear that such a house was used by the judge as a courtroom. Here are some examples:

The farm at Ilford Bridges was formerly used as the court house for Judge Jeffreys.

Judge Jeffreys held his assize at Ilford Bridges.

Altogether nine traditions of this sort were collected concerning this location alone. It may be the result of the building having been used as a local court in the past. Sometimes Jeffreys is said to have lived at certain places. This has been claimed for Stocklinch and Crickleaze on the Blackdowns. The court notion carried to its furthest extent becomes a form of folk etymology.

> Swell Court was so called because this was one of the many places where Judge Jeffreys held his assize. He was not at all bothered who he put to death. Other big houses farther away are called manors, because they did not have courts there.

Seven traditions collected associated Judge Jeffreys with the village of Stocklinch:

> During the last ten years there has died a man called Jeffreys Allen. It is thought that he was the last of the Judge Jeffreys family. The name had been changed round years before. This, the last one to die, decreed that he should be buried in a different churchyard from the rest of the family to show the shame of the family reputation.

The notion becomes established probably some years before by a local family that claimed ancestry from the judge. Tradition as a consequence produced the following:

> Judge Jeffreys was buried at the higher church. He was brought to Stocklinch at the dead of night. There was always a coffin in the vaults that was said to be his. This vault is now sealed over. It is known to be his coffin because it is shorter than the rest of them. He was brought headless, because he was beheaded in the Tower, so he was headless in his coffin.

A variation gives:

> Judge Jeffreys was buried in the church. He had come back to his manor, and being badly wounded, died there in hiding.

Jeffreys was born in 1648, at Acton Park, near Wrexham, and fast rose to fame. He was supported throughout the Bloody Assize by James, but when the latter fled, he tried to do likewise and was caught at Wapping, disguised as a sailor, and was sent to the Tower partly to save him from the mob. He died in the Tower and was buried there on 20 April 1689, but was removed to St Mary's Aldermanbury by order of Queen Mary three years later. Jeffreys's eldest son, John, was born in 1673 and died in 1702. He inherited his father's title, and on his death it became extinct. It is therefore unlikely that Stocklinch could ever claim direct descent from Jeffreys.

Another incident from the Bloody Assize that is still remembered with some bitterness is the conviction and hanging of Charles Speke at Ilminster along with eleven others:

> One of the Spekes was hanged, not because he was guilty of any murder but because during some war or other, when there was a war here, something to do with Somerset, he stopped back with a lady he knew and did not join his regiment, and was hanged on Toller Down.

A more correct version was given as:

> One of the Spekes was hanged for shaking hands with Monmouth when he came through Ilminster, as he knew him. He was of course sentenced by Judge Jeffreys. His brother however avoided being hanged by escaping.

George Speke, the father, was known to be friendly towards Monmouth, but at the time of the Bloody Assize he seems to have kept very quiet. John Speke, one of his sons, took part in the rebellion, but travelled abroad until the Restoration, and was finally elected MP for Taunton in 1695. The third son, Hugh, was ironically saved from the gallows by Jeffreys himself, who had previously tried him for sedition; rather than pay a fine Hugh had spent three years in the King's Bench Prison, where he was at the time of the rebellion—a forced confinement that probably saved his neck. He was, however, one of the chief transactors in the revolution of 1688. The only son left therefore was Charles, who by reason of the handshake was tried for being a conspirator in the rebellion. Jeffreys is reported to have stated, when asked if any special favour would be granted to a Speke, 'No, his family owe a life. He shall die for his brother, who is guilty of having been in the action, but has escaped.' Charles's last words were, 'I hope you will believe that I am not guilty as my judge and accusers have endeavoured to make me.' As he went, 'on every side of him, as well as up and down the town, the inhabitants were weeping and bewailing.' One even offered to die in his place. He was hanged in the Market Square, Ilminster, from an old tree.

*K.7. Smuggling*
The activities of smugglers have caught the imagination of the folk, and many places have become associated with them. Many of the traditions must date from the beginning of the eighteenth century when smuggling was at its height. The smuggler of popular romance is very different from the real thing. Smuggling was a violent business, involving bribery, perjury, informing, violence and murder. One Poole gang in 1748 attacked a customs house to regain a cargo of tea, previously taken from them. Later, two officers were captured, to stop them giving evidence; both died, one under the lash and the other when, after his eyes and nose were cut out, he was made to walk roped into a well and hang himself. Although smuggling decreased by the end of the century, runs were still made from Alderney, with landings at Beer, Lyme and farther up the Dorset coast. Goods would be sent inland probably via Axminster and so north across the Blackdown Hills to be sold in the prosperous Vale of Taunton, or in Dorset to Corfe Castle and Bere Regis, and so to Blandford and into the Blackmore Vale. Fiddleford Mill was a smuggling depot. Another route was from Poole and Christchurch inland to Kinson; from there the goods were taken to More Crichel, Thorney Down and so to Handley and Salisbury. Smugglers used pack horses and travelled at night. The occupation has left its mark on place names: Smuggler's Lane, Stourpaine, and Brandy Bridge, near Hatch Beauchamp, Somerset, to mention but two.

Traditions concerning smuggling are often vague. The Blackdown Hills are supposed to contain goods left by the smugglers en route for the Vale of Taunton. Another informant said that the smugglers used to hide their goods in some of the houses in Dowlish Wake. Sometimes the smugglers would use more subtle means:

The smugglers used to try and keep the people off the lanes. A coach was supposed to come up the street, a phantom coach. But the noise that was heard was in fact the smugglers about their illegal business.

A similar story is told of Winterborne Kingston, Dorset, where the smugglers are said to have dressed up as ghosts to frighten customs officials.[7] A widespread story explains the origin of the word 'moonraker'.

> Some smugglers were about to land their cargo of brandy when the customs officers were spotted. Afraid of being caught in possession of the barrels, they put them over the side of the boat, and marked the spot. The customs officers searched their boat, and went away disappointed. The smugglers then started to recover their valuable cargo, and did this by dragging the area with rakes. Meanwhile the customs officials, suspicious about the whole incident, had returned unawares. When challenged as to their behaviour, they pointed to the reflection of the moon, clearly visible in the sea, and said that they were trying to rake it out.

The story is not only told about smugglers. 'Moonraker' has come to mean a native of Wiltshire, and the story is sometimes told to their discredit, the situation being inland, the reflection being in a pond, and the guile employed by the smugglers omitted.[8]

In Dorset a famous smuggler, Gulliver, is still remembered:

> A band of smugglers used to come from Swanage and pass through Charlton Marshall. They came down Cemetery Lane, partly through Charlton Marshall and down River Lane. They were led by a man called Gulliver, who became so rich that he started a bank. His descendants still live in Charlton Marshall, probably where he lived, and are well off. The informant said that she had a ring that once belonged to Gulliver.

Gulliver was a Wiltshire man who organised a network of smuggling over several counties. By 1758 so many people were involved that it made the customs men's job very difficult. Gulliver settled at Thorney Down in about 1768. There a route led to Poole, and back to Salisbury via Handley. Ten years later he moved to Kinson so as to better organise his activities, and Thorney Down became a rendezvous. He later moved to Lyme Regis, retired at middle age and married a respectable banker's daughter, though this is only tradition. He certainly did live in great comfort in Wimborne.[9] His association with Charlton Marshall is not established.

# NOTES

## CHAPTER 1  SETTLEMENT AND DWELLING

1  Hutton, E. *Highways and Byways in Somerset* (1912), 377.
2  Camden, W. *A Chorographical Description of Great Britain and Ireland* (1586, revised and translated from the Latin, E. Gibson, 1722), 2nd ed, vol 1, Somerset, 69.
3  Boger, E. *Myths, Scenes and Worthies of Somerset* (1887), 35.
4  Walters, C. (ed). *Bygone Somerset* (1897), 116.
5  Poole, C. H. *The Customs, Superstitions, and Legends of the County of Somerset* (1877, 2nd ed, Guernsey, 1970), 123 .
6  Horstman (ed). *Nova Legenda Anglie*, Wynkyn de Warde, 1516, incl a translation of the life of St Decuman (Oxford, 1901), vol 1, 263–5.
7  Hulbert, Rev N. F. 'A Survey of Somerset Fairs', *Somerset Archaeological & Nat Hist Soc Proceedings*, vol 82, 129–30.
8  Hunt, R. *Cornish Folk-lore*, reprinted from *Popular Romances of the West of England* (1871, reprinted Truro, 1969), 18.
9  Ekwall, E. *Concise Dictionary of English Place Names*, 3rd ed (Oxford, 1951), under 'Allowenshay'.
10  Ekwall, under 'Sevenhampton'.
11  For literary source see Street, J. *Mynster of the Ile* (Taunton and Ilminster, 1904), 103.
12  *Somerset Life*, vol 2, no 3, 39ff.
13  Bett, H. *English Myths & Traditions* (London, New York, Toronto, Sydney, 1952), 123.
14  Radford, W. L. 'A Manorial History of Donyatt', reprinted from *Somerset County Herald*, 8
15  Street, *Mynster of the Ile*, 388.
16  See Udal, J. S. *Dorsetshire Folklore* (Hertford, 1922, 2nd ed, Guernsey, 1970), 212ff; and Dacombe, M. R. (ed). *Dorset Up Along and Down Along* (Dorchester, 1933), 102 and 103.
17  Tongue, R. L. *Somerset Folklore* (Folklore Society, 1965), 15.
18  *Somerset Proceedings*, vol 113, 1ff, special supplement.
19  Udal, *Dorsetshire Folklore*, 162
20  *Dorset Life*, vol 5, no 34, 21.
21  Tongue, *Somerset Folklore*, 103–4.

22 Mathews, F. W. *Tales of the Blackdown Borderland* (Somerset Folk Press, 1923), 91.
23 Hunt, R. *Cornish Folklore,* 31.


# CHAPTER 2 LIVELIHOOD AND HOUSEHOLD SUPPORT

1 Quoted by Sixsmith. *Staple Fitzpaine and the Forest of Neroch* (Taunton, 1958), from Polycraticus 1, para iv.
2 Shepton Mallet Gaol Register, 1876. Somerset Record Office.
3 Chafin, W. *Anecdotes and History of Cranborne Chase* (1818). Facsimile reproduction, printed Pitt Rivers (1886), 32–3.
4 Traill, H. D. (ed). *Social England* (1894), vol 2, 567.
5 Oliver, J. *Ancient Roads of England* (1936), 156.
6 *An Inventory of the Historical Monuments in Dorset,* 1 (West), HMSO (1952), 223


# CHAPTER 3 COMMUNICATION AND TRADE

1 Frazer, J. *The Golden Bough,* abridged ed (1949), 191.
2 Margary, I. D. *Roman Roads in Britain* (1955), vol 1, 113.
3 Hutchings, J. *The History and Antiquities of the County of Dorset* (1774), 3rd ed. Revised by W. Shipp and J. W. Hodson (1861–70), vol 4, 209.
4 Quoted by Udal, *Dorsetshire Folklore* (Hertford, 1922), 2nd ed (Guernsey, 1970), 132.
5 *Shorter Oxford English Dictionary,* under 'Pack'.
6 For these and other examples see Bett. *English Myths and Traditions* (1952), 49.


# CHAPTER 4 THE COMMUNITY

1 Collinson, Rev J. *History of Somerset* (Bath, 1791), 1, 38.
2 *Proceedings,* 112, 80.
3 Hunt, R. *Cornish Legends,* 46.
4 Tongue, R. L. *Somerset Folklore,* 101. Boger, E. *Myths, Scenes and Worthies of Somerset,* 559.
5 Child, F. J. *English and Scottish Popular Ballads* (Boston, 1857–9), 3, 9, line 120.

6 Briggs, K. M. and Tongue, R. L. *Folk Tales of England* (1965), 96–8.
7 Boger, E., 378
8 Hutton, E. *Highways and Byways in Somerset*, 288.
9 *The Victoria County History of Somerset*, vol 2, 24.
10 Calendar of Prisoners tried at Spring Assize held at Taunton 29 April 1879, *SRO*.

## CHAPTER 5  HUMAN LIFE

1 Tongue, R. L. *Somerset Folklore*, 100.
2 Brewer's *Dictionary of Phrase and Fable*, under 'red-haired person'.
3 Krappe, A. H. *The Science of Folklore* (1930), 210.
4 Quoted in *Proceedings, Dorset*, from *Travels through England of Dr R. Pococke, Bishop of Meath and of Ossory, in the years 1750–51*.
5 Poole, C. H. *Customs, Superstitions and Legends*, 123.
6 Poole, 123–6. Quoted by Poole from *Cornhill*, 1872.
7 Somerset Record Office.
8 See Chapter 9, J.11 etc.
9 Information from *Crockford's Clerical Directory, 1902* (1902), 'Dowlish Wake'.
10 I am indebted to Mrs H. M. Clarke for this.

## CHAPTER 6  NATURE

1 Grinsell, L. V. *The Ancient Burial Mounds of England* (1936), 2nd ed, 1953, 82.
2 Weinstock, M. B. *Old Dorset* (Newton Abbot, 1967), 62.
3 . . Tongue, R. L. *Somerset Folklore*, 23–4.
4 General traditions collected 1968–70, Somerset.
5 Chamber's *Biographical Dictionary*, under 'Charles I'.
6 Scorbutic: 'Of or pertaining to scurvy; symptomatic of or proceeding from scurvy', *SOED*.
7 Collinson, Rev J. *History of Somerset* (Bath, 1791), 10–12.
8 Horne, Dom E. *Somerset Holy Wells* (Somerset Folk Press, 1923), 37.
9 Ibid.
10 Tongue, 219.
11 Tongue, 27.

## CHAPTER 7 FOLK MEDICINE AND TIME

1 Oral Tradition—a tale that is still told locally, though see other versions in Poole, *Customs and Superstitions of Somerset*, 69ff, and Tongue, *Somerset Folklore*, 199.
2 Brewer's *Dictionary of Phrase and Fable*, under 'Cock crow'.
3 *The Standard Dictionary of Folklore, Mythology and Legend*, ed M. Leach and J. Fried (New York, 1949–50), under 'Cock'.
4 Brewer's *Dictionary*, under 'Cock'.
5 Opie, I. & P. *The Lore and Language of School Children* (Oxford, 1959), 1967, 267.
6 Opie, 268.
7 Opie, 269.
8 *Somerset Life*, vol 1, no 5, 7.
9 Brewer's *Dictionary*, under 'Ignis Fatuus'.
10 Tongue, 93–4.
11 Tongue, 29–30.
12 Matthews, F. W. *Tales of the Blackdown Borderland* (1923), passim.
13 Camden, W. *A Chorographical Description of Great Britain and Ireland*, revised and translated from the Latin, 1722. E. Gibson, 2nd ed, 1, 79.
14 Poole, *Customs*, 84.
15 Walters, C. (ed). *Bygone Somerset* (1897), 44.
16 Collinson, Rev J. *History of Somerset*, 3 vols (Bath, 1791), 2, 265.
17 Ibid.
18 Ibid.
19 Brewer's *Dictionary*, under 'Joseph of Arimathea'.
20 *Gentleman's Magazine* (1753).

## CHAPTER 8 POPULAR BELIEF AND PRACTICE

1 The tradition is also found in Dacombe, M. R. (ed). *Dorset Up Along and Down Along* (Dorchester, 1935), 105.
2 Newquay, Cornwall (c 1952).
3 Dacombe, 106. For other gipsy curses see Briggs, K. M. and Tongue, R. L., *Folk Tales*, 59.
4 *Proceedings*, Dorset, vol 31 (1910), 179.
5 Bett, H. *English Legends*, 41.
6 Legg, R. *A Guide to Dorset Ghosts* (Bournemouth, 1969), 12–13.

CHAPTER 9   MYTHOLOGICAL TRADITIONS, Part 1

1   Tongue, R. *Somerset Folklore* (Folklore Society Publications, 1965), 15.
2   Bett, H. *English Legends*, 68. Bett has a series of similar stories about the Devil throwing stones either at churches or in a competition, 69–70 and 77.
3   Briggs, K. M. and Tongue, R. *Folk Tales of England* (1965), nos 30 and 31. See also no 32. The Devil is also included in these tales.
4   Hunt, R. *Cornish Legends* (Truro, 1969), 16.
5   Bett, H. *English Myths and Traditions* (1952), 51; and Hutton, E. *Highways and Byways in Somerset* (1912), 258.
6   Grinsell, L. V. *The Ancient Burial Mounds of England* (1936), 2nd ed, 1953, 81.
7   Tongue, R. (1969).
8   Quoted in *Folklore* (1937), vol 48, 363.
9   The Merry Maidens near Burian, Dartmoor, were transfixed dancers who continued their revels into Sunday, piped by an evil spirit. Other examples of sabbath-breaking are Boscawen-un Circle, the Nine Maids at Stithians and St Columb Major, and the Hurlers near St Cleer. In the last example the activity was hurling not dancing. (See Hunt, R. *Cornish Folklore*, 25–6.)
10  For variations of these traditions and the following, 'The devil forming mounds', see Bett, H. *English Legends*, 70–2.
11  Lackington, J. *Life of Lackington*, 13th ed (1793), 327–8.
12  Tongue, R. op cit, 14.
13  Mathews, F. W. *Tales of the Blackdown Borderland* (Somerset Folk Press, 1923), 73–4.
14  Tongue, R. Lecture, Ilminster Girls' Grammar School (1966).
15  *SOED* under 'Hob' and 'Hobgoblin'.
16  Mathews, F. W. *Tales*, 68.
17  For further details see Legg, R. *A Guide to Dorset Ghosts* (Bournemouth, 1969), 30.
18  The last six black-dog traditions were collected by Mr R. W. Patten, 1970.
19  Miss Tongue mentions a similar tradition where the black dog is the result of a suicide or a corpse that fell out of a coffin and cracked its skull, allowing the ghost to escape. The location is the crossroads between Selworthy and Tivington. The story

as given here was supplied by Mr R. W. Patten, January 1972.

20  Legg, R., 28.

## CHAPTER 10  MYTHOLOGICAL TRADITIONS, Part 2

1  Tongue, R. *Somerset Folklore* (Folklore Society Publications, 1965), 100.

2  Grinsell, L. V. *Dorset Barrows*, Dorset Natural History & Archaeological Society (Dorchester, 1959).

3  For further examples of modern ghost lore see *Drive*, AA Magazine (autumn 1969), 141–3, nos 4, 9, 16, 26.

4  Munford, G. F. *Ghosts and Legends of South Somerset* (Somerset Folk Press, 1923), 20–30.

5  James, H. *The Portrait of a Lady* (1881; Penguin, 1963, 1967 ed), 578.

6  Street, J. *The Mynster of the Ile* (Taunton and Ilminster, 1904), 362.

7  Brewer's *Dictionary of Phrase and Fable*, 10th edn (1967), under 'Before you can say J.R.'.

8  Wheeler, H. *People's History of the 2nd World War* (September 1939–December 1940), 110–11.

9  Tongue, R., 129–30.

10  Tongue, 130–1.

11  Street, J., 387. See also Radford, W. L. 'A Manorial History of Donyatt', reprinted from *Somerset County Herald*.

12  See Mathews, F. W. *Tales of the Blackdown Borderland* (Somerset Folk Press, 1923), 25. Miss Tongue also has a version in *Somerset Folklore*, 14. There are some burial mounds on Cowleaze, near Milborne St Andrew, Dorset, where a golden coffin is said to be buried. Whenever people dig for it there is thunder and lightning.

13  *Proceedings*, Somerset, 5, i, 30ff.

14  Walters, C. (ed). *Bygone Somerset* (1897), 117.

## CHAPTER 11  HISTORICAL TRADITIONS

1  Walters, C. (ed). *Bygone Somerset* (1897), 59.

2  Page, W. (ed). *The Victoria County History of Somerset* (1906) gives the visit to Hinton House as taking place immediately before the Battle of Sedgemoor, but this is impossible as Monmouth

did not march that way, and only passed through Ilminster, collecting support as he went. The informant's oral tradition, however, probably takes the general view that the event happened on Monmouth's return in 1685.

3  *Proceedings*, Somerset, quoted from vol 73, 35.

4  Western Zoyland Parish Registers, quoted by Poole, C. H. *The Customs Superstitions and Legends of the County of Somerset* (c 1877), Guernsey, 1970, 104–6.

5  Street, J. *The Mynster of the Ile* (Taunton and Ilminster, 1904), 231. Information from MS 30077, British Museum.

6  *Proceedings*, Dorset, vol 5, 109.

7  Weinstock, M. B. *Old Dorset* (Newton Abbot, 1967), 63.

8  Rake, O. E. Racian. 'To proceed, make one's way, to walk, stroll, wander, now *dial*.' *SOED*. Grose: 'Some Wiltshire rusticks . . . seeing the figure of the moon in a pond, attempted to rake it out.'

9  Weinstock, M. B., 81.

# CLASSIFICATION OF ORAL TALES AND TRADITIONS

## A SETTLEMENT AND DWELLING

1       Local settlers
2       Derivations of names of villages and places
2.i     Local landowners and people
2.ii    Traditions of land tenure and organisation (churches, etc)
3       Fields, explanation of shape and size, etc, boundaries and fences
3.i     Common lands
4       Villages, growth, situations and buildings
5       Lucky or unlucky sites for houses, materials, traditions and building procedure
6       Household assets, fires, cupboards, sleeping accommodation, etc
7       House luck
8       Temporary dwellings
9       Buildings of the past
9.i     Stones and stone monuments, circles, stones with markings
9.ii    Giants' graves
9.iii   Stone seats and chairs
9.iv    Paths and tracks. (See C.1)
9.v     Earthworks, ditches and moats
9.vi    Earthworks, mounds
9.vii   Old buildings—secular
9.viii  Old buildings—religious
9.ix    Castles
9.x     Towers
9.xi    Burial grounds. (See E.10.vii)

9.xii    Other places where people have been buried, including crossroads

## B LIVELIHOOD AND HOUSEHOLD SUPPORT

1        Domestic selling and money-making
2.i      Hunting
2.ii     Poaching
2.iii    Highwaymen
2.iv     Piracy
3        Fishing
4
4.i      Livestock
4.ii     Wild animals
5        Agriculture and land culture
6        Trees, shrubs and plants
7        Traditions and occupations (including such things as thatching)
8        Lighting in the house
9        The fire
10       Food and drink
11       Personal habits

## C COMMUNICATION AND TRADE

1        Roads, paths or tracks
1.i      Tollhouses
1.ii     Bridges
1.iii    Fords
1.iv     Journeys
2        Travel by water
3        Beacons and larger communications
4
4.1      Money and commerce transaction
4.ii     Misers who hid hoards
5        Fairs, actual; markets

## D THE COMMUNITY

1        Foreigners and strangers

M

2      People engaged in work
3      Tyrannical masters, lazy servants
4      Dress
5      Society, mixing and social intercourse
6      The family
6.i    Derivations of surnames and others
7      Religion and the community
8      Church stories and legends of its religion
8.i    Churches changed from one site to another
8.ii   Ruined churches
8.iii  Haunted churches
8.iv   Unfinished churches
8.v    Churches built during day and knocked down at night
8.vi   Other religious ceremonies
9      Education and schools (including materials and books)
10     Legal systems and actions
10.i   Courts, trials and methods of proving guilty
10.ii  Punishments
10.iii Disposal of criminal bodies
10.iv  Crimes, including murder
11     Military service, and folktales of soldiers in community

## E HUMAN LIFE

1
1.i    The soul, external soul especially of giants, or in animals, especially the hare
1.ii   The soul after death
1.iii  External influences on the soul (stars, moon, etc)
2.i    The battle of the sexes
2.ii   Men and boys
2. iii Youth and age
2.iv   Man and woman—hussy, etc
3      Individual characteristics, dark/fair, tall/short, colour of hair, personal idiosyncrasies
4      People with special powers
5.i    Physical proportions, size, height, strength, smallness, fatness, etc

| | |
|---|---|
| 6 | Feats and contents involving bodily characteristics |
| 6.i | Strength |
| 6.ii | Endurance |
| 6.iii | Agility |
| 6.iv | Courage and daring |
| 7 | Marriage |
| 8.i | Conception and pregnancy |
| 8.ii | Childbirth |
| 8.iii | Abnormal births |
| 8.iv | Changelings |
| 8.v | Burial of infants |
| 9 | Sickness |
| 10 | Death |
| 10.i | Personification |
| 10.ii | Dying persons |
| 10.iii | The corpse |
| 10.iv | The wake |
| 10.v | The coffin |
| 10.vi | The funeral |
| 10.vii | The graveyard. (See also A.9.xi) |
| 10.viii | Manner of burial |
| 10.ix | Power of corpse |
| 10.x | The grave |
| 10.xi | Grave-robbing and robbers |
| 11.i | Return of the dead, circumstances and occupations |
| 11.ii | Returns to give help |
| 11.iii | Returns to gain help—release from purgatory, etc |
| 11.iv | Dead lover returns |
| 11.v | Dead arise before burial |
| 12 | Suicide |

## F NATURE

| | |
|---|---|
| 1 | Sun |
| 2 | Moon |
| 3 | Other heavenly bodies |
| 4 | The wind |
| 5 | Thunder |

| 6 | Bad weather or good |
|---|---|
| 6.i | Rain |
| 6.ii | Snow |
| 6.iii | Frost |
| 6.iv | Fog |
| 6.v | Rainbow |
| 7 | The four elements |
| 7.i | Fire |
| 7.ii | Water |
| 7.iii | Earth |
| 7.iv | Air |
| 8 | Natural features |
| 8.i | Rivers and streams |
| 8.ii | Waterfalls |
| 8.iii | Lakes |
| 8.iv | Rocks and stones |
| 8.v | Islands |
| 8.vi | Sea, including god of the sea |
| 8.vii | Bogs |
| 8.viii | Caves |
| 8.ix | Holes |
| 8.x | Underground passages |
| 8.xi | Hills and mountains |
| 9 | Wells |
| 9.i | Holy wells |
| 9.ii | Fairy wells |
| 10 | Woods and trees |
| 10.i | Personification in trees |
| 10.ii | Woods or forests |
| 11 | Herbs |
| 12 | Birds |
| 13 | Animals |
| 14 | Fish |
| 15 | Serpents |

## G FOLK MEDICINE

| 1 | Folk medicine cures |

## H TIME

| | |
|---|---|
| 1.i | Day |
| 1.ii | Night |
| 1.iii | Midnight |
| 1.iv | Dusk |
| 1.v | Dawn, cock crow, etc |
| 1.vi | Specific times of importance or periods of time |
| 2 | Local festivities, dates |
| 3 | Pilgrimages (times) |
| 4 | Special festivals |
| 4.i | May (spring) |
| 4.ii | Midsummer |
| 4.iii | Hallowe'en |
| 4.iv | Christmas |
| 4.v | Twelfth Night |

## I FOLK TALES INVOLVING POPULAR BELIEF AND PRACTICE

| | |
|---|---|
| 1 | Owners, ownership and change in ownership, possession |
| 2 | The first and the last |
| 3 | Direction |
| 4 | Participation and sympathetic magic, etc |
| 5 | Fate |
| 6 | Divination |
| 6.i | Dreams |
| 6.ii | Omens |
| 6.iii | Predictions |
| 7 | Individuals credited with supernatural powers |
| 7.i | Healers |
| 7.ii | Saints |
| 7.iii | Prophets, seers and wise men |
| 7.iv | Vicar or priest |
| 7.v | Seventh son or posthumous son |
| 7.vi | Women |
| 8 | Talisman, efficacious for various things |
| 9 | Sorcery and witchcraft |
| 9.i | Sacrifice |

9.ii    Offerings
9.iii   Person surrendering himself to the Devil
9.iv    Sorcery for discovering guilt
9.v     Magic
10.i    Crosses
10.ii   Numbers
11      Speech
11.i    Curses
11.ii   Charms
12      Right and wrong
12.i    Sacrifice (holy)
12.ii   Interference with fairy world
12.iii  Interference with the supernatural
12.iv   Taboos, including undesirable places
12.v    Dishonesty

## J MYTHOLOGICAL TRADITIONS

1       Origins
1.i     People and first settlers. (See A.1)
1.ii    Natural features—terrestrial and heavenly bodies (including meteorites)
1.iii   Other natural features, eg sea, rivers, lakes
1.iv    Rocks and stones
1.v     Topographical features, eg mountains, tunnels, etc
2       Supernatural beings
2.i     Devils, appearances and associations
2.ii    Demons
2.iii   Witches
2.iii.a Black
2.iii.b Grey
2.iii.c White
2.iv    Giants
2.v     Mythological champions and warriors
2.vi    Wizards
3       Fairies
3.i     Origin
3.ii    Visibility

| | |
|---|---|
| 3.iii | Form and appearance |
| 3.iv | Food |
| 3.v | Dwelling |
| 3.vi | Occupation and behaviour |
| 3.vii | Fairy fairs |
| 3.viii | Fairy mischief |
| 3.ix | Fairy wealth |
| 3.x | Fairy hunt, or race |
| 3.xi | Fairy games |
| 3.xii | Fairy help |
| 3.xiii | Fairies and living people |
| 4 | Fairy places |
| 4.i | Houses |
| 4.ii | Moats |
| 4.iii | Circles |
| 4.iv | Paths |
| 4.v | Hills |
| 4.vi | Palaces |
| 4.vii | Underground chamber |
| 5 | Abduction by fairies |
| 6 | Fairy lover |
| 7 | Fairy wind |
| 8 | Misled by fairies |
| 9 | Fairy stroke (illness caused by fairies) |
| 10 | Spirits, Will o' the wisp, etc |
| 10.i | Spirits of natural places—woods, trees or a tree, rivers |
| 10.ii | House spirit, hob |
| 10.iii | Spirits banned or deterred |
| 10.iv | Male spirits |
| 10.v | Female spirits |
| 10.vi | Animal spirits |
| 10.vii | Pixies |
| 11 | Ghosts |
| 11.i | Meetings with ghosts |
| 11.ii | Ghosts as youths |
| 11.iii | Ghosts as men |
| 11.iv | Ghosts as women |

11.v    Headless body
11.vi   Spectral coach
11.vii  Spectral funerals
12      Specific ghosts known by name
13      Sub-human beings
14      Supernatural water creatures
15      Serpents and dragons
16      Supernatural places
16.i    Countries and islands
16.ii   Towns and cities
16.iii  Houses under water
16.iv   Supernatural castles and houses
17      Hidden treasure
17.i    Origin
17.ii   Nature of it
17.iii  Guardian
17.iv   Dream of treasure-diggers
17.v    Adventure of treasure-diggers
17.vi   Stories about hidden treasure
18      Other supernatural phenomena
18.i    Sounds
18.ii   Lights
18.iii  Objects
18.iv   Blood
18.v    Ship and boats
18.vi   Sky and weather
18.vii  Supernatural rationally explained
19      Afterworld
19.i    End of the World
19.ii   Day of Judgement
19.iii  Heaven
19.iv   Hell
19.v    Purgatory

## K HISTORICAL TRADITIONS

1       Individual personages
2       Particular families

3      Poets
4      Persons of local fame
5      Historical events
5.i    Colonisation
5.ii   Local migration
5.iii  The Romans
5.iv   The Danes or other invaders
5.v    Normans
5.vi   Civil War
5.vii  Monmouth and Judge Jeffreys
5.viii Recent events
6      Local calamities or events of note
7      Smuggling
8      Popular historical traditions of Wessex

## L RELIGIOUS TRADITIONS

1      God
2      Angels
3      Christ and Virgin
4      Apostles

# BIBLIOGRAPHY

Books cited or consulted. The place of publication is London unless otherwise stated.

Aarne, A. and Thompson, S. *The Types of the Folktale: A Classification and Bibliography* (Folklore Fellows Communications, no 180) (Helsinki, 1961)

Anonymous. *An Historical Account of the Heroick Life and Magnanimous Actions of the most Illustrious Prince, James, Duke of Monmouth* (1683)

*A Review of the Arguments in Favour of the Continuance of Impeachments notwithstanding a dissolution.* By a Barrister (1791)

*The Western Martyrology or Bloody Assizes*, 5th edn (1705)

Arkell, W. J. *The Geology of the Country around Weymouth, Swanage, Corfe and Lulworth* (HMSO, 1947)

Aubrey, J. *Brief Lives*, ed Clark, A. (1898) (2 vols)

*Remaines of Gentilisme and Juaisme* (1687, reprinted by Folklore Society, 1880)

Baring-Gould, S. *Lives of the Saints* (1872, rev edn, 16 vols, 1914)

Bett, H. *English Legends* (London, New York, Toronto, Sydney, 1950; reprinted 1952)

*English Myths and Traditions* (London, New York, Toronto, Sydney, 1952)

Boger, E. *Myths, Scenes and Worthies of Somerset* (1887)

Bovet, R. *Pandaemonium or the Devil's Cloyster* (1684)

Brailsford, J. W. *Hod Hill*, vol 1 (Trustees of the British Museum, 1962)

Burne, C. S. *The Handbook of Folklore* (Folklore Society Publication, 1913, reprinted 1957)

Butler, Rev A. *Lives of the Saints* (Dublin, 1883)

Camden, W. *A Chorographical Description of Great Britain and Ireland.* (Revised and translated from the Latin, 1722, E. Gibson. 2 vols, 2nd edn)

Chafin, W. *Anecdotes and History of Cranborne Chase* (1818. Facsimile reproduction printed by Lt-Gen Pitt Rivers, 1886)

Challoner, Bishop. *Britannia Sancta* (1745)

Child, F. J. *English and Scottish Popular Ballads* (Boston, 1857–9, 8 vols)

Colby, F. J. (ed) *Visitations of the County of Somerset, in the year 1623* (1876)

Collinson, Rev J. *History of Somerset,* 3 vols with index (Bath, 1791)

Dacombe, M. R. (ed) *Dorset Up Along and Down Along* (Dorchester, 1935)

Davidson, J. *British and Roman Remains, near Axminster* (1833)

Douch, R. *A Handbook of Local History, Dorset* (University of Bristol, 1952)

Ecles, F. C. *St Decuman's,* with a life of St Decuman by G. H. Doble (Williton and Minehead, 1932)

Fea, A. *King Monmouth* (London and New York, 1902)

Frazer, J. *The Golden Bough,* abridged edn (1949)

Gasquet, F. A. *The Black Death,* 2nd edn (1908)

Gray, Hinton St George. *Whitelackington and the Duke of Monmouth,* reprinted *Som Arch Soc Proc,* vol LXXIII (1927)

Greswell, W. H. P. *The Forest and Deer Parks of Somerset* (1905)

Grinsell, L. V. *The Ancient Burial Mounds of England* (1936, 2nd edn, 1953)

*Dorset Barrows* (Dorchester, 1959)

Hinchy, F. S. *The Heart of Dorset* (Gillingham, nd)

*Blandford, Today and Yesterday* (Blandford, 1960)

HMSO. *The Hampshire Basin, and Adjoining areas,* British Regional Geography, 3rd edn (1960)

HMSO. *An Inventory of the Historical Monuments in Dorset,* vol 1, West Dorset (1952)

Hoehling, A. A. & M. *The Last Voyage of the 'Lusitania'* (1957, 1959 edn)

Horne, Dom E. *Somerset Holy Wells* (Somerset Folk Press, 1923)

Hortsman, Ed. *Translation of the Life of S Decuman,* as printed in *Nova Legenda Anglie,* Wynkyn de Warde (1516, vol 1; Oxford, 1901)

Hunt, R. *Cornish Folklore,* reprinted from *Popular Romances of the West of England* (1871, reprinted Truro, 1969)

*Cornish Legends*, reprinted from *Popular Romances of the West of England* (1871, reprinted Truro, 1969)

Hutchings, J. *The History and Antiquities of the County of Dorset* (1774, 3rd edn, 4 vols. Revised by W. Shipp and J. W. Hodson, 1861–70)

Hutton, E. *Highways and Byways in Somerset* (1912)

Irving, H. B. *Life of Judge Jeffreys* (1898)

James, H. *The Portrait of a Lady* (1881; Penguin, 1963, 1967 edn)

Knott, O. *Old Dorset* (Poole, 1958)
*Witches of Wessex* (Dorchester, 1958)

Krappe, A. H. *The Science of Folklore* (1930)

Lackington, J. *Life of Lackington*, 13th edn (1793)

Legg, R. *A Guide to Dorset Ghosts* (Bournemouth, 1969)

Margary, I. D. *Roman Roads in Britain*, 2 vols (1955)

Mathews, F. W. *Tales of the Blackdown Borderland* (Somerset Folk Press, 1923)

Muddiman, J. G. (ed) *The Bloody Assizes* (Edinburgh and London, 1929)

Munford, G. F. *Ghosts and Legends of South Somerest* (Somerset Folk Press, 1922, 2nd edn, 1922)

Oliver, J. *The Ancient Roads of England* (1936)

Opie, I. & P. *The Lore and Language of School-Children* (1959, 1967 edn)

O'Suilleabhain, S. *A Handbook of Irish Folklore* (Folklore Associates, Inc, Hatboro, Pennsylvania, 1963)

Oswald, A. 'Country Houses of Dorset', *Country Life* (1935; 2nd edn, 1959)

Page, W. (ed) *Victoria History of Somerset*, 2 vols (1906)

Poole, C. H. *The Customs, Superstitions and Legends of the County of Somerset* (1877, 2nd edn, Guernsey, 1970)

Powys, L. *Somerset and Dorset Essays* (1957)

Pulman, G. P. R. *The Book of the Axe* (1854)

Radford, W. L. 'A Manorial History of Donyatt', reprinted from *Somerset County Herald*

Rattenbury, J. *Memoirs of a Smuggler* (Sidmouth and London, 1837)

Richmond, I. *Hod Hill*, vol 2 (Trustees of the British Museum, 1968)
Robinson, W. J. *West Country Manors* (Bristol, 1930)
Roscoe, E. (ed) *Marnh'll Book* (Gillingham, 1952)
Sixsmith, R. A. *Staple Fitzpaine and the Forest of Neroch* (Taunton, 1958)
Smart, T. W. W. *A Chronicle of Cranborne* (1841)
Street, J. *The Mynster of the Ile* (Taunton and Ilminster, 1904)
Sydenham, G. F. (ed), Cameron, A. J. *The History of the Sydenham Family* (East Molesey, 1928)
Tatlock, J. S. P. 'The Dragons of Wessex and Wales', The Mediaeval Academy of America, Mass. Offprint from *Speculum, a journal of Mediaeval Studies*, vol 8, no 2 (April 1933)
Thompson, S. *The Folktale* (New York, 1946)
Tongue, R. L. (ed), Briggs, K. M. *Somerset Folklore* (Folklore Society, 1965)
Tongue, R. L. & Briggs, K. M. *Folk Tales of England* (1965)
Tongue, R. L. *Forgotten Folk Tales of the English Counties* (1970)
Traill, H. D. (ed) *Social England*, 5 vols (1894)
Truman (ed). *Somersetshire Country Houses and Villages* (1931–2)
Udal, J. S. *Dorsetshire Folklore* (Hertford, 1922, 2nd edn, Guernsey, 1970)
Walters, C. (ed) *Bygone Somerset* (1897)
Watson, W. G. W. (ed) *Calendar of Customs, Superstitions, Weather Lore, of the County of Somerset*, reprinted from *Som Co Herald* (1920)
*Somerset Life and Character* (Somerset Folk Press, 1924)
Weinstock, M. B. *Old Dorset* (Newton Abbot, 1967)
Wyatt, A. J. (ed) *An Anglo-Saxon Reader* (1919, 1965 edn)


*Dictionaries and Directories*
*Brewer's Dictionary of Phrase and Fable*, Brewer, E. C. (1870, 10th edn, 1967)
*Burke's Landed Gentry*, Burke, J. (1849); 8th edn, vol 2 (1894); 15th edn, ed H. P. Gordon (1937)

*Calendar of Prisoners tried at Spring Assize, held at Taunton Tuesday 29 April 1879* (Taunton, 1879)

*Chambers's Biographical Dictionary*, Thorne, J. O. (ed) (1897, 1964 edn)

*The Clergy List for 1872* (1872)

*Complete Baronetage*, ed G.E.C. vol 5 (Exeter, 1906)

*Complete Peerage*, ed G.E.C. Rev V. Gibbs & Lord H. de Walden, vol 7 (1929)

*Concise Oxford Dictionary of Place Names*, Ekwall, E. (3rd edn Oxford, 1951)

*Crockford's Clerical Dictionary, 1902* (1902)

*Dictionary of British Folktales*, Briggs, K. M. Part A. (2 vols) Folk narratives. Part B. (2 vols) Folk legends (1970)

*Dictionary of British Surnames*, Reaney, P. H. (1958)

*English Place Name Elements*, Smith, A. H. (ed) English Place-Name Soc (Cambridge, 1956)

*Shepton Mallet Gaol Register, 1876*, Somerset Record Office

*Somerset Incumbents*, Weaver, F. W. (ed) (Bristol, 1889)


*Magazines and Periodicals*

*Devon Life*, ed A. C. W. King, vol 5, no 32

*Drive*, AA magazine (autumn 1969)

*Gentleman's Magazine*, vol 8 (July 1738)

*Musgrave's Obituary*, ed Armytage, G. J. Printed for Harleian Soc (1901), vol 5

*Somerset Life*, ed J. K. Dryden, vol 1, no 5; vol 2, no 7; vol 2 no 8

*Walford's Antiquarian*, Walford, E. (ed), no 61, vol 40, January 1887 (1887)

*Proceedings of the Dorset Natural History & Archaeological Society*, published annually since 1877

*Proceedings of Somerset Archaeological & Natural History Society*, published annually since 1849, Taunton. Index to vol 1 to 20 (1876)

*Somerset and Dorset Notes and Queries*, published quarterly since 1890

# ACKNOWLEDGEMENTS

I wish to thank the following, whose help and guidance have been invaluable.

The many informants in Somerset, Dorset and other areas who provided information; Mr S. F. Sanderson, the Director of the Institute of Dialect & Folklife Studies, University of Leeds, and his colleagues; the students of my General Studies Course, Blandford School, 1969/70; Mr R. W. Patten, for many useful traditions; the staff at Blandford Public Library; Somerset Archaeological & Natural History Society; Somerset Record Office; Mrs M. F. Palmer and Mrs P. Taylor, for proof-reading; Mr B. Winkle, for printing photographs; Mrs H. M. Clarke, for typing; Folklore Associates, Detroit, Michigan, for the classification system.

# INDEX

This index concentrates on listing geographical locations. Subject headings are included only if they do not figure obviously in the classification system. A general subject heading should therefore be found in this classification system and then its presence located in the book.

Abbotsbury, 34
Agglestone, 106
Aldborne, 35
Aller, 148–9
Allowenshay, 15, 45
Almer, 139
Arthur, King, 70, 155–7
Ash, 112
Ashill, 74, 77–8, 117
Athelney, 148
Athelstan, 53
Avalon, 156
Axminster, 37, 162, 166
Axmouth, 37

Babb, Master, 49–50
Badbury Rings, 157
Badger Street, 16
Barnwell (Camb), 53
Barrington Court, 160
Barrington Hill, 158
Barrington Priory, 132
Batcombe, 63
Bath, 37, 81, 96
Bedivere, Sir, 156
Beer, 166
Bellmoor, 21

*Beowulf*, 70
Bere Regis, 149, 166
Bethlehem, 92
Bettiscombe Manor, 98–101
Bettiscombe skull, 98–101
Bickenhall, 140
Bindon Abbey, 74
Bishop's Lydeard, 126, 133
Bishop's Wood, 24
Black Bess, 33
Black Death, 48
Black dog, 36, 39, 126–8
Blackdown Hills, 16, 19, 29, 30, 37, 110, 122, 126, 128, 164, 166
Black Gates, 103, 137
Blackmoor Vale, 166
Blandford Bridge, 36, 127
Blandford Forum, 22–3, 95, 126, 130, 140, 141, 146, 150, 159, 166
Bloody Assize, 162–5
Bloody Shard Gate, 29, 159
Bodmin, 110
Bodmin Moor, 70
Bolsover, 17
Boscastle, 21

Braunton (church), 47
Bread, 34
Brendon Hills, 16, 88
Bridges, 36, 135
Bridgwater, 116, 162
Bristol, 42, 96, 163
Bristol Channel, 133
Broadway, 21, 48, 97, 112, 117, 143, 158
Brunanburgh, 53
Bryanston Ho, 94, 111, 139
Buckland Hill, 143
Buckland St Mary, 128
Buckland, West, 90

Cadbury Hill, 157
Camelot, 157
Cannard's Grave, 26
Castle Cary, 50
Castleton, 71
Castle Neroche, 106, 109, 112, 126, 149, 151–2, 157, 158
Cat, 116
Cerne Abbas, 77, 118–19
Chaffcombe, 70, 90, 127
Changed site, 44–9
Chard, 50, 55, 95, 132, 143, 160, 162
Charles I, 76, 91
Charlton Marshall, 74, 139, 167, 168
Charborough Ho, 19, 63
  Lion Lodge, 19
  Park, 18, 63
Checkendon, 44
Cheselborne, 24, 106, 108
Chesil Beach, 33, 96

Child Okeford, 16
Chilton Cantelo Ho, 98
Chilworthy, 142
Chink, 103, 123, 137–8
Chinnock, 85
Chipping Norton, 107
Chiselborough, 85–8
Christchurch, 166
Churchstanton, 108, 112, 113, 140
Cider, 30, 34, 38, 51
Cirencester, 37
Cityford, 19
Civil War, 43, 150
Clayhanger Ho, 122
Cock, 36, 83, 108
Combe St Nicholas, 24, 95, 97, 112, 115, 122
Combe Sydenham, 153–4
Corfe, 129, 139, 140, 152–3
Corfe Castle, 106, 166
Cornwall, 48, 98, 107, 109, 142, 157
Cothelstone, 75, 133, 134
  Well, 75–6
Cranborne, 134
Cranborne Chase, 28
Crediton, 20
Crewkerne, 14, 15, 74, 123, 140
Cricket Malherbie, 72, 128, 136
  Court, 72, 137
  Cross, 43, 137
Crickleaze, 164
Crick Stones, 109
Crimchard, 112

Cromwell, 17, 158–9
Cudworth, 74, 137, 151
Culm Davy, 151
Curry Mallet, 49, 122

Danes, 58–9, 133, 134, 148–9
Dartmoor, 25, 32, 42
Day of Judgement, *see* Judgement
Delcombe Manor, 74, 135
Dillington, 78, 137
Dinnington, 37
Dommett, 126
Donhead St Andrew, 129
Donyatt, 21, 52, 74
Dorchester, 163
Dowlish, East, 45–6, 52, 67, 74, 88, 121, 122, 137–8, 143, 166
Dowlish Wake, *see* Dowlish, East
Dowlish, West, 21, 45–7
Dowsborough Camp, 134, 149
Dozmere Pool, 70
Drake, 48, 153–4
Dundry, 16
Dunster Castle, 148
Durweston, 21, 71, 124–5

Easenton, 19
Eastbury Ho, 141, 144–5
Ettricke, 62
Etymology (folk), 16, 17, 41, 164
Exeter, 20, 37, 57, 163
Excalibur, 70
Exmoor, 88, 111, 116, 126

Fairies, 40, 46, 49, 104, 120, 139
Fairs, actual, 40–2, 85–8
Fiddleford, 73, 166
Fisher Way, 37
Forde Abbey, 74, 160
Fosse Way, 37
Fox, 116

Gains Cross, 138
Gamekeepers, 28–9, 159
Gawain, Sir, 156
*Gawain and the Green Knight*, 14
George, 11, 140
Giants, 106, 107, 110, 118–19; *see also* Cerne Abbas and Grave
Glastonbury, 77, 89–92, 156, 157
Golden Cap, 34
Golsoncott, 142
Grail, 91
Graves, giants', 24–5, 107, 108 Ordinary, 25–6, 64–6, 159; *see also* Cannard's Grave, Mary Hunt, Merland's Corner, Nan Bull
Gulliver, 167

Hair, red, 58–9
Hallowe'en, 59, 84, 86–8, 121, 139, 147
Ham Hill, 117
Hambrook, 144
Hambledon Hill, 21, 79, 158, 159
Handley, 134, 166, 168

Hanford Ho, 132
Hatch Beauchamp, 166
Hawkridge, 107
Hare, 116, 118
Hellstone, 106
Hemyock, 144
Henry I, 156
Henry II, 156
Henry VIII, 53, 139, 145
Hercules, 119
Highwaymen, 30–3
Hilcombe, 21, 149–50
Hinton Ho, 20, 95–6, 111, 121, 141, 142, 160
Hinton Park, 20, 95, 141
Hinton St George, 39, 84–8, 111, 118, 123, 126, 160
Hod Hill, 21, 127, 158
Holcombe (Mendips), 48, 139
Holman Clavel Inn, 122–3
Honiton, 37
Horner Mill, 128
Horton, 78
Houghton, 40, 73
Hurdlestone, 105

Ilchester, 51
Ilford Bridges, 163
Ilminster, 18, 25, 39, 55, 67, 89, 137, 143, 149, 150, 158, 160, 162, 163, 165, 166
Ina, King, 53
Isle of Wight, 106
Iwerne Minster, 125

Jack o' Lantern, 120–1, 87–8
Jack White, 50

Jeffreys, Judge, 144, 160, 162–5
Journeys, 36–40
Joseph of Arimathea, 90–1, 156
Judgement, Day of, 61, 84, 88

Ker Moor, 148, 149
Keynston, 142
Kielder Moor, 111
Kilmersdon, 94
Kingstone, 45
Kinson, 166, 168

Lady of the Lake, 70
Lambert's Castle, 110
Lambrook, 64
Landowners, 17
Langton, 141
Lidmarsh, 128
Limington, 51
Lincoln, 37
Lion Lodge, *see* Charborough, 19
Littlecote, 144
Liverpool, 20
Long Sutton, 86
Lopen, 51, 84–7
  Head, 33
Ludney, 66
Lulworth, 63
  Cove, 158
  West, 26, 73
Lynton, 108
Lyme Regis, 166, 168
Lytchett, 142

Maldon, Battle of, 134
Manton, 25
Markets, 40–2; see also Fairies
Martock, 51
Marshwood Vale, 98
Mary Hunt, 25, 57, 82
Mary Hunt's Grave, 25
Maypole, 119
Merland's Corner, 26
Merlin, 109
Merriott, 60, 150
Merryfield, 77
Milborne St Andrew, 174
Milton Abbas, 19, 74
Milton Abbey, 74, 135
Milverton, 133
Minchinhampton Stone, 108
Minehead, 116
Monmouth, rebellion, 15, 43, 72, 158–62
Moolham, 160; see also Dowlish West
Moonraker, 35, 167
Monksilver, 144
Montacute, 54
More Crichel, 166
Muchelney, 52, 53
Mules, F. M., 68

Nailsea, 157
Nan Bull (Grave), 26
Neroche, see Castle
Nettlecombe Tout, 25
New Year's Eve, 58
Nimmer, 90
Norton Fitzwarren, 20, 148–9

Okeford Fitzpaine, 16, 51, 97
Old Christmas Day, 88–9, 91
Old Christmas Eve, 89
Other World, 83, 127, 139
Otterford, 129
Oxenford, 16; see also Dowlish, West

Pack Monday Fair, 40
Parrott, river, 53, 71
Paulett, Sir Amais, 51
Perranporth, 135
Pilgrims, 37
Pinney, 100
Pimperne, 80, 126, 127, 139, 159
Piracy, 33–4
Pitminster, 114
Pitt, 18
Pixy, 58; led, 40; see also Fairies
Plague, 42, 48
Plymouth, 20
Plympton, 20
Poaching, 27–30, 159
Pocock, 32
Poltergeist, 121, 123–5
Pontypool 87, 88
Poole, 20, 142, 166, 168
Popham, 144
Porlock, 107, 126
Portesham, 106
Portland, 102, 106
Portman (Viscount), 94
Puckington, 74
Punkie, Night, 84–8
Purbeck Hills, 158

Purtington, 137

Quantock Hills, 75, 133

Rabbit, 102, 109, 116
Racedown, 100
Ragged Dick, 108
Raven, 80, 94
Red Post, 51
Ringwood, 162
Roadwater, 142
Rollright Stones, 107
Romans, 83; *see* K.5.iii, 157

Sacrifice, 36
St Agnes, 75
St Agnes's well, 75–6
St Audries, 126
St Brannock, 47
St Carantoc, 148
St Cyprian's well, 78
St Decuman, 13, 14, 64, 76
St Dunstan, 34
St Gabriel, 34
St Michael's Hill, 54
St Michael's Mount, 107
St Nipperham's well, 78
St Piran, 15
St Rayn, 14
St Rayn Hill, 14
Salisbury, 126, 163, 166, 168
    Market, 42
Saturnalia, 89
Sea, 150
Seaweed, 34
Seavington St Michael, 17, 64
Sedgemoor, 15, 32, 160–2

Selworthy, 128, 173
Semley, 98, 101
Settlers, 14–17
Sexton, 34
Shaftesbury, 145, 150
Shapwick, 35
Sheep-stealing, 28–30
Sherborne, 40
Shillingstone, 16
Simons Burrow, 110
Sixpenny Handley, 16
Skipperham well, 77–8
Skivertons well, 78
Skivvers well, 77
Skulls, 60, 98–101
Somerset & Dorset Railway, 95
Somerton, 133, 139
South Petherton, 33, 71
Speke, B., 68, 138, 143, 160, 162
Speke, family, 67–8, 165
Spettisbury, 116
Spunkies, 88, 121
Stanton Drew, 107, 109
Stanton St Gabriel, 34
Stathe, 115
Staple Fitzpaine, 16, 105, 109–13, 151
Stickland, *see* Winterborne Stickland
Stocklinch, 17, 122, 164, 165
    Ottersey, 76
Stogursey, 126
Stoke sub Hamdon, 108
Stoke Pero, 88, 121
Stonehenge, 108, 109

Stones, 42, 47–8, 97, 104–13, 151
  Sarsen, 104
Stour (river), 71, 73, 111
Stourpaine, 21, 120, 127, 166
Stubhampton, 141
Studland, 106
Sturminster Newton, 134–6, 138, 145
  Castle, 73, 135
Swainswick, 81
Sydenham, E., 153
Sydenham, G., 144, 154

Tarr Steps, 111
Tarrant Keyneston, *see* Keynston
Tarrant Gunville, 29, 127, 141, 149, 159
Tavistock, 42
Taunton, 20, 55–7, 157, 162, 163, 165
Thorney Down, 166–8
Tintagel, 157
Tisbury, 53
Tivington, 173
Tolpuddle Martyrs, 51
Tower of London, 94
Trent Barrow, 71
Twelfth Day, 88, 89
Turpin, 33

Uplyme, 126

Wadeford, 34, 157–8
Wake Hill, 39, 103, 137, 142–3, 160

Walditch, 77
Wareham, 139
Washford, 142
Watchet, 13, 14, 19, 64, 76, 133
Weacombe, 126
Wellington, 108, 110, 144, 158
Wells, 75–9, 163
West Buckland, *see* Buckland, West
West Dowlish, *see* Dowlish, West
Weston Zoyland, 162
Westport, 126
Weymouth, 163
Whitechurch Canonicorum, 34
Whitelackington, 16, 74, 158, 160–1
Whitestaunton, 74, 76, 90, 142, 158
Whittlestone, 108
Will o' the wisp, 88, 120–1
Wilscombe, 144
Wilton, 42
Wimblestones, 108
Winsford Hill, 126
Wimborne, 62, 95, 140, 149, 168
Winchester, 163
Windwhistle, 30–1, 33, 37, 60, 79, 113, 130, 137, 140–1
Winterborne Clenston, 73
Winterborne Houghton, *see* Houghton
Winterborne Kingston, 132, 167

Winterborne Stickland, 146–7

Wirral, 90

Wolsey, Cardinal, 51

Wood Court, 74, 78, 123, 142, 151

Wookey Hole, 107

Wookey, witch of, 107

Wool, 26, 74

World's End, 139

Wyke Regis, 147

Yew trees, 61, 79